BREAKDOWN

BREAKDOWN

How the Secret of the Atomic Bomb Was Stolen during World War II

Richard Melzer, Ph.D.

Sunstone books may be purchased for educational, business, or sales promotional use. For information please write: Special Markets Department, Sunstone Press, P.O. Box 2321, Santa Fe, New Mexico 87504-2321.

FIRST EDITION

10 9 8 7 6 5 4 3 2 1

Library of Congress Cataloging-in-Publication Data:
Melzer, Richard.
    Breakdown: how the secret of the atomic bomb was stolen during World War II / Richard Melzer.—1st ed.
        p. cm.
    Includes bibliographical references and index.
    ISBN: 0-86534-304-7
    1. Los Alamos Scientific Laboratory—Security measures. 2. Atomic bomb—New Mexico—Los Alamos—History. 3. Manhattan Project (U.S.)—History. I. Title.

QC789.2.U62 M45 1999
355.8'25119'0973—dc21   99-052053

Published by SUNSTONE PRESS
              Post Office Box 2321
              Santa Fe, NM 87504-2321 / USA
              (505) 988-4418 / orders only (800) 243-5644
              FAX (505) 988-1025
              www.sunstonepress.com

To Dad,
a strong, loyal soldier in the Pacific
who survived World War II to become
the strong, loyal father of our family

CONTENTS

PREFACE

On the afternoon of April 12, 1945, President Franklin D. Roosevelt died suddenly at his vacation home in Warm Springs, Georgia. By 7:09 that evening Vice President Harry S. Truman was sworn into office as the nation's thirty-third president during a hastily assembled ceremony held in the Cabinet Room of the White House.[1]

Moments later Secretary of War Henry L. Stimson privately briefed the new chief executive on "an immense project that was under way—a project looking to the development of a new explosive of almost unbelievable destructive power."[2] The "new explosive" was the atomic bomb. The "immense project" was the Manhattan Project, the code name for an undertaking kept so secret that not even the country's vice president had known of its existence prior to assuming the presidency.[3]

Truman later said that in becoming president it "felt like the moon, the stars, and all the planets had fallen on me."[4] Undoubtedly, much of that great weight represented Truman's new-found knowledge of a weapon "of almost unbelievable destructive power" for which he was now responsible. Within three months, President Truman would make one of the most difficult, momentous decisions in all of history: to use the atomic bomb against two Japanese targets and precipitate the end of World War II.[5]

It was possible to keep even the vice president of the United

States unaware of the Manhattan Project and its mission because great efforts had been made—and much money had been spent—to keep the project the best kept secret of World War II. That was no easy task. Begun in August 1942, the Manhattan Engineer District consisted of thirty-seven installations in nineteen states, with major operations at Oak Ridge, Tennessee (code named Site X); Hanford, Washington (code named Site W); and, most significantly, Los Alamos, New Mexico (code named Site Y).[6]

In fact, it was widely believed that no place in the world was more heavily guarded than Los Alamos. Security was tightest there because Site Y was where dozens—and later hundreds—of American and British scientists had gathered for the duration of World War II, or until they had beaten the nation's fascist enemies in perfecting an atomic bomb.[7] Although officially an ally of the United States in the war, the Soviet Union and its agents were scrutinized as much, if not more, than the Germans, the Japanese, or any other declared enemy of the era 1941 to 1945.

The history of how American and British scientists beat the Axis powers and the Soviet Union in the race to develop an atomic bomb has been told many times, with emphasis on the breakthrough scientific achievements of this massive effort.[8] Much less has been said about the huge security challenge of keeping news of scientific developments at Site Y in, while keeping overly curious foreign agents out. What measures did Site Y's tight security include, and how strictly were they enforced by military and civilian personnel assigned to Los Alamos and its environs? And, once established, how successful was the vast security net placed over Los Alamos and its (mostly) dedicated inhabitants from March 1943, when Site Y opened, to July 1945, when the product of Site Y's labor was finally dropped on Japan to end the war in the Pacific and World War II overall?

For years these questions were addressed in passing by historians in monographs, by scientists in their memoirs, and by the commander of the Manhattan Project, Leslie R. Groves, in his autobiography. Los Alamos and its top secret operation also captured the vivid imaginations of authors and film producers, becoming the often-distorted focus of many spy novels and Hollywood movies in the decades since World War II.[9]

Two electrifying developments have brought security at Los Alamos to the center of national and international attention once more. First, the collapse of the Soviet Union and its menacing intelligence agency, the Komitet Gosudarstvennoy Bezopasnosti (KGB), sparked the writing of many new books authored by former KGB agents and others with access to formerly-closed KGB archival records.[10] Much of what historians have long believed about security at Los Alamos during World War II must be reconsidered in light of the often startling revelations found in this literature—if and when it is believed. Second, and even more recently, news of Chinese espionage at the Los Alamos National Laboratory in the 1980s and 1990s has sent shock waves through the U.S. intelligence community. Following Congressional and Department of Energy investigations, Energy Secretary Bill Richardson has concluded that a "total breakdown" in security at the lab has occurred.[11]

Perhaps the answers to historical questions regarding security at Los Alamos during World War II can help address many of the pressing issues regarding security at Los Alamos today. If so, history will have served its noblest mission: to help guide our decisions in the present based on the knowledge and wisdom we glean from the past.

I have learned much from the past and have been able to complete this work thanks to the kind help of mentors, friends, and colleagues, including Professor Ferenc Morton Szasz (who helped get a young graduate student on the right academic track years ago), historians Nelson Van Valen and Julie Van Valen (who read the manuscript and made countless astute suggestions), and Lieutenant Colonel Wes Martin (who read the manuscript from an experienced security expert's point of view). Judy Bowyer Martin also read the manuscript with the skills of an expert proofreader. Reinaldo Garcia, Cindy Chavez, and Teresa Valverde lent technical support. My research would have been impossible without Roger A. Meade at the Los Alamos National Laboratory archives, Hedy Dunn, Patricia F. Goulding, and Theresa A. Strottman at the Los Alamos Historical Society archives, and Kris Warmoth, Kris White, Wayne Oakes, and Judy Marquez of the University of New Mexico—Valencia Campus library. In addition, many veterans of the Manhattan Project generously shared their time and memories, including John Lansdale, David Hawkins, McAllister Hull, Lawrence Antos, Eleanor (Jerry) Stone Roensch, Arno Roensch, Marian Jacot, Louis Jacot, Edward F. Hammel, and Carl W. Buckland, Jr. As always, James Clovis Smith, Jr., at Sunstone Press was most encouraging and helpful. Finally, Rena, Rick, Kam, and my parents have been supportive, patient, and cheerful—key elements in the pleasure, completion, and possible success of any writing project.

—Richard Melzer
Belen, New Mexico

1
THEORY

"The security restrictions [at Los Alamos] have been more rigid than on any other portion of the entire Manhattan Project."
                                        Lieutenant Colonel Stanley L. Stewart
                                                        August 18, 1945[1]

Lieutenant Colonel Stanley L. Stewart's words, uttered within days of the Japanese surrender on August 15, 1945, were widely believed in the United States military and in the nation as a whole at the end of World War II. Without the tightest security at Los Alamos, how could the United States have secretly developed a highly technical nuclear weapon at the cost of millions of dollars and the labor of thousands of loyal Americans? How could the product of this labor have been dropped on Hiroshima (August 6, 1945) and Nagasaki (August 9, 1945) in acts that rivaled the Japanese attack on Pearl Harbor for surprise and nerve at the outset of World War II in 1941? Security at Los Alamos must have been ironclad indeed to produce such remarkable results in just twenty-eight short months, March 1943 to July 1945.

Site Selection

Security at Los Alamos began with its selection in November 1942 as the best of several western sites considered for the location of a secret lab to invent and produce an atomic bomb. It was clearly favored by Manhattan Project leaders J. Robert Oppenheimer, a University of California physicist chosen to lead the scientific community at Site Y, and Brigadier General Leslie R. Groves, the military commander chosen to oversee the entire Manhattan operation as of September 23, 1942.[2] Oppenheimer and Groves favored Los Alamos for several good reasons.

First, Los Alamos was isolated. Formerly an exclusive boys school set 7,200 feet above sea level on the Pajarito Plateau of northwestern New Mexico, Los Alamos was removed from population centers but relatively close to major transportation routes; the small Indian pueblo of San Ildefonso lay eight miles to the east and the Hispanic village of Espanola lay eighteen miles to the northeast. The nearest railhead, at Santa Fe, lay forty-two miles to the southeast, while the nearest airport, at Albuquerque, lay sixty miles further on. Los Alamos could be reached from only two directions, with main access up a treacherously winding road that reminded one traveler of an ascent into the foreboding mountains of Tibet; riding down this perilous route reminded a second traveler of a wild amusement park ride often experienced by passengers "with eyes closed, and white, white knuckles from holding the seat in front."[3] Such a remote location allowed for scientific experiments and the noisy testing of explosives far removed from the prying eyes and ears of unwelcome observers. High on a mesa two miles wide and eight miles long, Los Alamos could also be easily guarded against enemy espionage, sabotage, and military attack. Distant from the Atlantic and Pacific coasts, Los Alamos was less vulnerable to detection by the Japanese from the west, by the Germans from the east, or by Soviet agents from the east or west.[4]

Site Y's isolated location gave U.S. security personnel the additional advantage of carefully scrutinizing resident scientists on a relatively confined, 54,000 acre mesa. On one level, top scientists and their families had been recruited from major universities and labs to help facilitate the exchange of information and better coordinate the early completion of an atomic weapon. But on a security level, often loquacious scientists had been brought to Los Alamos to make sure they did not intentionally or unintentionally share secrets about their work with overly inquisitive strangers. Accustomed to reporting their experimental findings and conclusions at scientific conferences and in academic journals, the demands of tight security and secrecy were new and uncomfortable to many scientists at Los Alamos. In fact, some scientists saw their remote mesa (usually referred to as The Hill) as a place to keep them and their advanced ideas *in* as much as a place to keep enemy spies *out*. European scientists who had escaped probable confinement in German concentration camps were most prone to recognize The Hill as a virtual prison where people often vanished for years with little contact with the outside world. Only half facetiously, some believed that a better name for Los Alamos was Lost Almost.[5]

Recruitment of Scientists

J. Robert Oppenheimer forewarned scientists of the need for tight security and secrecy when he recruited them to live and work at Site Y. A memorandum sent to prospective scientists told of certain amenities of life on The Hill, such as varied outdoor activities and pleasant weather, but added that security would be strictly enforced, making it necessary "to rupture completely our normal social associations with those not on the project"; the memo itself was marked "restricted," meaning that its contents were not to be freely discussed with others.[6] But Oppenheimer did not want to frighten potential workers away. With nuclear scientists "the country's scarcest labor commodity," and an estimated 315 physicists needed for all high priority projects in 1943, the challenge was to candidly warn scientists of security restrictions at Site Y without scaring them (and their families) off.[7] The best way Oppenheimer could put it in 1943 was that "we shall all be one large family doing vital work within the wire."[8]

Oppenheimer met with mixed success. Of the original thirty-three scientists recruited, only fifteen agreed to work at Los Alamos.[9] Many agreed with Leo Szilard of the Chicago Metallurgical (Met) Lab that "Nobody could think straight in a place like that. . . . Everyone who goes there will go crazy."[10] Despite such dire predictions, Oppenheimer's recruitment record improved with time, especially when many eminent scientists joined his team, often bringing an entourage of colleagues, graduate students, and valuable scientific equipment with them from their former labs at Berkeley, Princeton, Chicago, Purdue, and elsewhere.[11] But recruitment remained one of Oppenheimer's greatest problems throughout the war. Unable to find enough civilian experts, Manhattan Project leaders arranged for young, qualified soldiers to be transferred from Army units across the country. Most were men with strong engineering, scientific, or technical backgrounds prior to entering the service; many were graduate students who had not yet completed their advanced degrees when they were drafted or volunteered for military service. The first thirty-nine members of this Special Engineer Detachment (SED, 9812th Technical Service Unit) arrived at Site Y in late 1943. By mid-1944 almost a third of the scientific staff were SEDs. At war's end this highly respected detachment numbered about sixteen hundred.[12] As many as fourteen hundred specially selected members of the Women's Army Corps (WAC) were similarly recruited to serve as staff members, if not scientists, starting with a detachment of only seven in April 1943.[13]

Oppenheimer would have had additional difficulties in recruiting scientists to The Hill if General Groves had carried out his original plan to make all Manhattan Project scientists into military officers. The general believed that giving scientists Army commissions would help establish a chain of command (with Oppenheimer as their colonel), instill discipline, and improve security overall. In short, Groves hoped to control his civilian scientists just as he controlled his own troops. A product of West Point (graduating fourth in the class of 1918) and a career officer, Groves had developed a well-deserved reputation for completing large projects, including the construction of the War Department's Pentagon complex just prior to his assignment to the Manhattan Project. A no-nonsense, by-the-book military man, he had little understanding of, no less patience for, civilian workers, including most civilian scientists. Groves thought of most scientists as intellectual snobs. He alienated many of them in an early Manhattan Project meeting by insisting that although he lacked a Ph.D., "I think you should know that after I left West Point I spent ten years doing nothing but studying. No outside jobs, no teaching—just ten years of pure study. Now, that should be about equal to two Ph.D.s shouldn't it?"[14] Declaring that he didn't care if the scientists in his charge liked him, Groves asserted that his only objective was "to have things running well," not to win popularity contests with the civilians he described as longhairs, prima donnas, and "the largest collection of crackpots ever seen."[15]

The best General Groves could say about most scientists was that they were "temperamental people" who "detested the [military] uniform" and did everything possible to make his life "hell on earth."[16] The worst Groves could say was that "If this were a country like Germany, . . . there were a dozen [scientists] we should have shot right off. And another dozen we could have shot for suspicion and carelessness."[17] If the general had had his way, all scientists would have worn signs around their necks like the one that hung on the wall in his Washington, D.C., office: "O Lord! Help me to keep my big mouth shut!"[18] Unable to appreciate the scientists' academic culture, Groves attempted to transform them by forcing them into his military culture—with its strict security regulations and punishments— by giving them commissions as officers in the U.S. Army.

At first, Oppenheimer complied with Groves' wishes, going so far as to order his officer's uniform and taking an Army physical at the Presidio in San Francisco.[19] But key scientists balked at the idea of militarizing the planned lab at Los Alamos. Robert F. Bacher of Cornell, Isidon I. Rabi of Columbia, Robert R. Wilson of Princeton,

Louis W. Alvarez of the University of California, and Hans Bethe of the Massachusetts Institute of Technology were among those who were "horrified" by Groves' intentions, arguing that to be effective and creative in their thinking scientists needed the freedom to disagree with one another at all times. This freedom would be severely limited if junior officers felt they could not challenge the authority of higher-ranking officers, including Oppenheimer himself.[20] Militarization would also "make the exchange of ideas much too formal, and hence too slow," in Bethe's words.[21] Finally conceding to these objections, Groves grudgingly agreed that Site Y's technical lab would remain in civilian hands until the atomic bomb was built, at which time Los Alamos would become a completely military operation.[22] Charles L. Critchfield refused to join the Los Alamos staff when Oppenheimer and Edward Teller approached him in late 1942 until he was assured in 1943 that his family could live with him and that he and his colleagues "didn't have to be majors in the Army."[23] At least one scientist remained so skeptical and adamantly opposed to military control that he submitted his resignation from the Manhattan Project effective the day the Army took over. Such a transition never occurred, and Robert Bacher never felt compelled to resign for this reason.[24]

Security Clearance Procedures

Once recruited, all Site Y personnel and their accompanying families underwent a thorough security clearance process. Detailed questionnaires asked for information about one's relatives, schools, military service (including which country's military), membership in organizations since 1930, employment since 1935, and foreign countries visited (with reasons for each visit) since 1935. The names and addresses of three references were also needed to complete this government form.[25]

Most scientists and staff members were scrupulous in their answers. Charles Hjelmgren, a Swedish-born resident of Chicago, listed the Chicago Swedish Male Chorus among his organizations, while Devona Perry listed the Kings Herold, an innocent church organization to which she had belonged since childhood. Unfamiliar with this group, security officers questioned Perry about the Kings Herold "in great detail."[26] MacAllister "Mac" Hull, a SED from LaGrange, Illinois, recalled that even the librarian for whom he had worked in high school was questioned when he listed her as a reference on his security clearance form.[27] Security checks could take as long as a month for scientists like Edward Hammel, although Hammel had been working on highly sensitive atomic research at Princeton University for two years prior to his transfer to New Mexico in 1944.[28]

Potential personnel could be denied security clearance for several main reasons. Those who tried to cover up major (or minor) criminal records were usually denied clearance, although the need for men with particular skills could influence final decisions. However, no exceptions were made if a person had been convicted of rape, arson, or narcotics charges. "Such persons," wrote Groves in his memoirs, "were felt to be unreliable because of their demonstrated weakness in moral fiber and their liability to blackmail" by foreign agents.[29]

But of all the reasons for being denied security clearance, association with a Communist or Communist front organization was the most important, according to Colonel John Lansdale, Jr., the Army officer responsible for security in the Manhattan Project as a whole. Lansdale recalls two or three scientists from the University of California who were denied clearance for this reason, especially after Oppenheimer told Lansdale that one of them was "quite a Red." Giovanni Rossi Lomanitz, a young Berkeley physicist thought to have questionable political ties, was not only denied security clearance to come to Los Alamos, but was also denied a draft deferment. Lomanitz was promptly drafted into the Army where he and his political ideas were considered less of a threat than in the politically sensitive labs of Berkeley or Los Alamos.[30]

Intelligence officers may have been justified in their evaluation and treatment of Lomanitz, but they were clearly inaccurate in their appraisal of physicist Arthur Holly Compton of the Met Lab in Chicago. The Army's investigation of Compton had supposedly revealed that he had "been associated with certain Communist-front organizations." Security officers refused to approve Compton, concluding that "We must not have in such a key position a man about whose loyalty there is a shadow of a doubt." Only after Colonel Lansdale "took pains to acquaint himself personally" with Compton was the confusion about the scientist's background cleared up. Ironically, Compton was cleared in November 1943 when, he later recalled, "the most critical aspects of my assignment [in the Manhattan Project] were already completed."[31]

Arrival in Los Alamos

Those who cleared the security clearance hurdle faced the often mysterious experience of traveling to Los Alamos from points across the nation and, in the case of British scientists, overseas. Various methods were used to keep Site Y's location a secret during these travels. Richard Feynman and his colleagues from Princeton, New Jersey, were told "not to buy our train ticket[s] in Princeton . . . because Princeton was a very small station, and if everybody bought train tickets to Albuquerque, New Mexico, in Princeton there would be some suspicions that something was up" in or around Albuquerque. Ever the maverick, Feynman bought his ticket in Princeton anyway because he reasoned that if his colleagues bought their tickets elsewhere, his lone ticket purchase would neither attract attention nor compromise secrecy. He was right, of course, unless everyone in his group jumped to the same conclusion.[32]

Enrico Fermi's wife, Laura, remembered her first railroad trip to New Mexico quite well. Traveling without her husband, she was relieved to see an old friend and well-known scientist on the same train with her. Aware that they were instructed not to reveal where they were headed, Laura Fermi and Harold Urey talked of many things en route west, "but neither of us mentioned our destination or the purpose of our trip." They simply got off at Lamy, New Mexico, and were "whisked away" in separate cars to Los Alamos, fifty-odd miles further north.[33]

Military personnel often believed that they were headed overseas to the Pacific when they received orders to travel west from posts back East. Some, like Mac Hull, were given a packet of envelopes and ordered to travel by train in small groups. At each train stop they were to open the next designated envelope, call the telephone number written inside, report that they were safe, and proceed to the next stop where the process would be repeated. In this fashion, Hull and his seven companions completed their odyssey from Oak Ridge, Tennessee, to Lamy without incident.[34]

From Lamy newcomers were transported in soldier-driven cars to 109 East Palace Avenue, a stone's throw from the centuries-old Spanish plaza in Santa Fe. There they found a small, adobe-walled office with only one regular employee, Dorothy S. McKibbin. Years later McKibbin wrote that

> Most of the new arrivals were tense with expectancy and curiosity. They had left physics, chemistry, and metallurgical laboratories, had sold their homes or rented them, had deceived their friends, and then had launched forth into an unpredictable world. They walked into 109 East Palace expecting anything and everything, the best and the worst.[35]

Only McKibbin's calming influence reassured most scientists and their wives, despite long journeys and frayed nerves. One of Oppenheimer's favorite, most trusted staff employees, McKibbin efficiently arranged for transportation "upstairs" to the scientists' final destination, The Hill.

Main Gates and Security Passes

After their memorable first drive up The Hill, newcomers passed through the main east gate (designated Gate #1), about a mile from the outskirts of their new "hometown." A seldom-used back gate (designated Gate #3) was available for those entering from the far less direct route into Site Y from the west. Most entered without incident, although even high-ranking officers could face trouble on this final leg of their journey. When Navy Captain William S. "Deak" Parsons first arrived in June 1943, the guards on duty refused to let him and his family pass through Gate #1. Instead, a Military Police-man (MP) called his sergeant and excitedly declared, "We've really caught a spy! A guy down here is trying to get in, and his uniform is as phony as a three dollar bill. He's wearing the eagles of a colonel and claims that he is a captain." The confusion was cleared up when the MP's sergeant explained that a Navy captain's insignia (the first to be seen at Los Alamos) was much different than an Army captain's. The newly enlightened, slightly embarrassed guard finally waved Deak Parsons and his weary family into Los Alamos.[36]

Parsons and all other newcomers over the age of six were soon issued security passes that they were required to show each time they entered or left Los Alamos. At least one corporal and two privates inspected all passes at the main gate onto the site. Gate passes included photo IDs, descriptive information (such as identifying "scars or oddities"), each person's signature, and, eventually, each resident's fingerprints.[37] European-born scientists objected to fingerprinting in particular. According to Eugene Wigner, a Hungarian scientist at Los Alamos,

> A fingerprint record might someday fall into the hands of the Nazis. I had no doubt that if the Germans won the war they would swiftly begin rounding up everyone in the Manhattan Project for execution. And the rounding up would go easier with fingerprints.[38]

European exiles were also reminded of the authoritarian regimes they had left behind when cars were searched on an irregular basis at Gates #1 and #3. Even those who sought U.S. citizenship were in-convenienced by the pass system. Emilio and Elfriede Segre were made to take their citizenship exams in the guard post at Gate #1 because the federal examiner sent to question them lacked a pass to enter Site Y.[39]

Sentries assigned to check passes at perimeter gates were usually courteous and competent, although stories soon circulated about seemingly unreasonable demands made by "one small clique of MPs [who] resented the civilians bitterly and did all they could to make life miserable for them." Their attitude, according to Eleanor Jette, was "What makes you [scientists] so . . . precious that you need to be guarded?"[40] Other MPs were simply overly scrupulous. When five-year-old Ellen Bradbury smashed her thumb at play, her father, Norris E. Bradbury, attempted to get her to the nearest hospital to their home in Frijoles Canyon. The nearest hospital was in Los Alamos, but because only her father, as a top official at the lab, had a gate pass, Ellen was refused entry into Site Y. Ellen was only granted permission to proceed to Site Y's small hospital after her father made several phone calls to military authorities who undoubtedly recalled that General Groves had "moved heaven and earth . . . to obtain the transfer of Lieutenant Commander Norris Bradbury to this project."[41] Following a similarly frustrating experience, a scientist's wife concluded that regulations governing passage into Los Alamos "top[ped] any screwy regulations of an Army post anywhere."[42]

Security Briefings

Newcomers on The Hill attended required security briefings (some said indoctrinations) within days of their arrival. Security briefings were often conducted by Peer de Silva, Site Y's military head of security for most of the war. In an unusual career path, de Silva had entered the U.S. Army as a private in July 1936, only to be discharged one year later to enter the U.S. Military Academy in 1937. Graduating from West Point in 1941, he rose through the officer ranks, becoming a captain shortly before being assigned to the Manhattan Project in October 1943.[43] De Silva was described as young and even "debonair," although, as their most direct contact with the military and the restrictive rules that governed their lives, many scientists neither liked nor trusted him.[44] The physicist who lived closest to de Silva at Los Alamos used words like "smooth," "icy," and "slick" to describe the security officer.[45] Even Site Y's Security Committee, consisting of civilians David Hawkins, John H. Manby, and Joseph W. Kennedy, complained about poor communications between civilian and military personnel, although de Silva had been specifically brought to Los Alamos "to work more closely with the Security Committee in the Technical Area."[46]

Captain de Silva began each newcomers' briefing by reading the Espionage Act of 1917, reminding his listeners that "all information concerning the Project is classified information, [the] dissemination of which is [a punishable] offense." All in attendance signed a document to confirm that they had heard and understood the meaning and seriousness of this law.[47] The remainder of de Silva's briefing was just as stern. Robert Y. Porton remembers that the lecture "impressed me very much. . . . [The officer] said, 'What these people are doing here can shorten the war by at least a year. My advice to you is do the job to which you are assigned. Don't ask questions. Don't talk.'"[48]

Captain de Silva described Site Y's security measures in some detail. His elaborate briefings were reenforced in a restricted security manual given to each resident and on the pages of *The Daily Bulletin*, a regular, one- to two-page news sheet printed on site from the spring of 1943 to the project's conclusion. Even *The Daily Bulletin* enjoyed a blanket of security: its masthead always included the warning that "THIS PAPER IS PUBLISHED FOR THE SITE—KEEP IT HERE!"[49] The same plea for secrecy was repeated on posters hung throughout Los Alamos and at the start of movies shown in on-site theaters.[50]

Censorship Rules and Box 1663

Captain de Silva's briefings, Site Y's security manual, *The Daily Bulletin*, posters, and movie trailers emphasized the great need for secrecy in all communications, starting with private correspondence. As of late 1943, mail to The Hill was officially censored. Scientists had suspected that their mail was being censored since shortly after the first contingent of civilians arrived in Los Alamos in the spring of 1943. To test these suspicions, Emilio Segre mailed a letter to his wife in Los Alamos while he was away on a trip to the "outside world" in mid-1943. Segre carefully placed a strand of hair in the letter's envelope, but when his wife opened it, the hair was gone. Segre and his colleagues believed that this was all the evidence they needed to prove that their mail had been tampered with by military censors.[51]

In response to frequent complaints regarding censorship, General Groves denied knowledge of the practice, but promised to investigate. His official investigation resulted in a denial nobody seriously believed. Skeptical as ever, the scientists volunteered to have their mail censored as of December 1943, if only so they would know the rules and would no longer feel that they were being duped by Groves and his security staff at Site Y. Reportedly, Los Alamos became the only military post in the continental United States to experience censorship for the duration of World War II.[52]

Censorship rules were quite specific. Correspondents were never to mention where they worked, the nature of their work, the equipment they used, the names of their fellow workers or neighbors, the distance to various locations (near and far), or even the picturesque scenery that surrounded their isolated site. Photographs enclosed in correspondence could not show buildings, equipment, signs, or local scenery for fear that visual evidence or natural landmarks could be identified by foreign agents. Cameras, in fact, had to be registered and locked in specified safes on site. Codes were forbidden, as were letters written in languages other than English, Spanish, French, German, Italian, Polish, Russian, Norwegian, or Swedish unless a written translation was enclosed. A long list of terms were strictly taboo, including "atomic," "uranium," "fission," "chemist," and, especially, "physicist." Scientists with Ph.D.s were never to be referred to as "professors" or "doctors," but simply as "misters."[53]

Finished letters were to be placed in unsealed envelopes so that censors had easy access and those who received such correspondence would not suspect that they were reading already- opened, censored material.[54] Only close relatives were sent official notification cards explaining that all mail was censored. Family members were to sign and return the cards they received "with the understanding that you will not disseminate [information about censorship] beyond your immediate family."[55] Completed letters were to be mailed in "receptacles provided for such purposes on the Post" and never in "Post Office facilities in adjacent communities."[56]

As many as eighteen censors worked in quarters located upstairs in the U.S. Post Office building in Santa Fe. Each censor was assigned an examiner number (2030 to 2039, 2295 to 2299, and 3051 to 3053) which was stamped on the envelopes of all approved letters. Experts in their field, censors did not hesitate to return problematic letters, noting infractions and insisting that all objectionable words or phrases be removed.[57] Most were legitimate requests, but scientists still complained that the censoring process delayed mail (up to forty-eight hours) and that some requests were far-fetched and unreasonable. In one instance, Bernice Brode's correspondence was returned when she drew small round faces with smiles and frowns on a letter. According to the censor, Brode's letter was "returned to sender because . . . unusual markings may not be passed."[58]

As a gifted, albeit irreverent young theoretical physicist, Richard Feynman had many run-ins with censors when he corresponded with his wife, Arlene, a TB patient living at the Presbyterian Sanatorium in Albuquerque while Feynman lived and worked in Los Alamos.

One of Arlene's pastimes was to create codes and use them in letters to her husband. Feynman, an amateur cryptologist, enjoyed the challenge of breaking Arlene's coded messages. Upset by this family game, Army censors demanded a key to each of Arlene's codes so that they could read her letters and understand their meaning. Feynman at first refused, but eventually compromised: Arlene would send the code for each letter and the censors would use it to decipher her message, but they would not send the code's key to Richard so that he could have the fun of figuring it out himself. The arrangement worked well until Arlene sent Feynman a shopping list of things she wanted Richard to buy her (such as litharge and glycerine to mix a cement), but the censors objected that it was a new code she had devised without enclosing the required key. They complained to Feynman, who contacted Arlene and soon realized the cause for the confusion. The Feynmans enjoyed a revenge of sorts by including a coded message on the back of a jigsaw puzzle on one occasion and dropping Pepto Bismol powder in a letter (so that it would spill over the censor's lap) in a later prank.[59]

Incoming mail was also censored to make sure that outsiders did not know (or guess) Site Y's location and purpose. When a librarian at the National Research Council in Washington, D.C., wrote to a friend at Site Y "that she had an idea as to what was going on at Los Alamos," military authorities called in the letter's recipient and asked her about the librarian and her knowledge of Los Alamos. Mildred Richards defended her correspondent, saying that the "most subversive act" in the librarian's life was joining the Daughters of the Confederacy. Richards surmised that the librarian had deduced "what was going on [at Site Y] from the scientists who used [her] library and subsequently went to Los Alamos."[60]

While some censors seemed unreasonable, others were cooperative and, in fact, helpful. In one case, a Los Alamos resident sent a letter and referred to an enclosed check. An alert censor reportedly returned the letter to its sender, noting that the promised check was missing and "politely chiding the sender for his absent-mindedness."[61]

In this instance, the sender was grateful, but most scientists continued to resent the imposition of censorship and the loss of yet another freedom. As Jane S. Wilson wrote, it was never "a pleasant or easy thing to surrender one's rights as an American citizen," especially when security officers were accused of being "almost always inconsistent, often high-handed, and sometimes unjust."[62] At least one letter writer expressed his discontent by including nastier and nastier jokes in his mail, hoping to disgust his censors into provocation. Alan U. Hershey requested information from the Soviet Philatelic Society just to shock the censors. Others simply poked fun at their censors, as in a skit performed at Fuller Lodge, a main social gathering place at Los Alamos. The skit's props included a small box for outgoing mail and a huge box labeled "Returned by Censor."[63]

To prevent a suspicious increase in the number of new post office box addresses in the Santa Fe area, all incoming mail for scientists and their dependents was to be addressed to a single 6"x11" post office box in the Santa Fe general post office: the famous Box 1663.[64] As the official address for so many residents, Box 1663 became the location given for both mundane and significant events in the scientists' lives. Robert and Kitty Oppenheimer's daughter, Katherine, was one of many babies "born" in Box 1663 during the wartime baby boom at Los Alamos. Eighty married couples listed Box 1663 as the birthplace on their babies' birth certificates during the project's first year alone; an average of ten more were "born" in Box 1663 each month for the rest of the war.[65] Far less momentously, a major catalog company was said to object to so many requests for catalogs from a single post office box. The company reportedly wrote a letter to Box 1663, declaring, "We have sent over a hundred catalogs to this address and will send no more."[66]

Telegrams and the few telephones in operation in Los Alamos were likewise monitored. Groves preferred phone calls to written communications for security reasons; he was known to make hundreds of calls per day, including as many as five per day to Oppenheimer at Site Y. The general was, nevertheless, disturbed by the use of phones by scientists. After monitoring phone conversations in Los Alamos and discovering too much "loose talk" among scientists, Groves fired off several letters to Oppenheimer, naming names and insisting that Oppenheimer clamp down on the scientists in question.[67]

Long-distance calls were routed via Denver for fear that the large volume of calls to Los Alamos would tip off diligent spies that something big was happening at this remote locale. No phone directories were published for security reasons and because no directory could keep up to date with daily additions and changes. Phone operators memorized numbers or relied on frequently revised typewritten sheets. Among the most used and best remembered office telephone numbers were Oppenheimer's (#146), Parsons' (#147), and the pass desk (#104). There were few home or public pay phones for most of the war. When long-distance emergency calls came in, "the called party would be notified in person by the MPs," according to former operator Jerry Stone.[68] Only English was permitted to be spoken in phone conversations, and "if a speaker's voice trailed off a little, the censor [was known to] testily cut in with 'Speak louder, please!'"[69]

Other Freedoms Compromised

Security measures reached into the scientists' personal lives in ways that surpassed precautions taken at any other Manhattan Project site. Even marriage ceremonies were well guarded. As many as thirteen weddings of couples employed at Site Y took place at Dorothy McKibbin's Santa Fe home. McKibbin later recalled that an armed guard stationed at the end of her driveway stopped every car that drove down her dirt road, including McKibbin's neighbors'.[70] "Security was so tight," said McKibbin, "that the minister did not know the names of those who were to be married until he arrived at [each] ceremony."[71]

Married couples and all other residents could attend religious services held regularly in Los Alamos. Services were provided for the convenience of church goers, but also to eliminate another need to travel off The Hill and become conspicuous new members on church rolls in Santa Fe and its surrounding communities. An Army chaplain, Captain Matthew Imrie, reported for duty in August 1944 to help handle this spiritual/security need.[72] Site Y's small hospital served a similar purpose, reducing the need for scientists and their families to go to Santa Fe's hospitals and thus draw attention to the admission of famous scientists or their relatives as patients. If patients died, local "coroners were discouraged from filing detailed reports of the circumstances."[73]

At home, married couples were not to discuss "the gadget" that consumed so much of the scientists' waking hours. Most wives guessed, but seldom knew, what the product of their husbands' labor might be, other than that it promised to shorten the terrible war still raging overseas. Eleanor Jette recalled her husband Eric looking preoccupied after a typical day in the lab. Eric Jette stretched out on a couch in his living room where he "studied the nailholes in the ceiling while he pondered the problems ahead of him behind an impenetrable wall of silence."[74] Secrecy created considerable tension in some families. When Phyllis Fisher kiddingly suggested that she and her husband, Leon, name their unborn child Uranium Fisher, "Leon roared at her never to mention that word again and clapped his hand on her mouth when she protested."[75]

Technical books and journals even vaguely pertaining to nuclear research were banned from the shelves of home libraries. To prevent enemy agents from compiling data on Los Alamos personnel from subscriber lists, scientific journals had to be forwarded from former university or lab addresses to either Box 1663 or a designated mail drop (Post Office Box 5370) in the Los Angeles, California, general post office. Scientists who sought to publish articles "pertinent to the problem at hand" had to secure approval from Site Y's security office, although an affirmative approval was highly unlikely, to say the least. Even scientific articles written prior to the creation of this approval process were matters of concern to intelligence officers. When Emilio Segre's article entitled "Artificial Radio-activity and the Completion of the Period System of the Elements" appeared in the July 1943 issue of *Scientific Monthly*, Captain de Silva expressed trepidation in a memo to Oppenheimer, although he realized that Segre had written the article while still on the faculty at the University of California and not yet a scientist at Los Alamos. Those who sought patents for their discoveries in physics, chemistry, metallurgy, ordnance, explosives, and electronics could expect similar reactions. A complex method of recording inventions was established by a separate Patent Office in Los Alamos, organized by Major Ralph Carlisle Smith after July 1943.[76]

On a far more intrusive level, concealed microphones were placed in the scientists' offices and private residences to record conversations. At least one woman recalled a visit by intelligence officers who questioned her about her neighbors' activities. After the war, Colonel Lansdale admitted that other methods of Army surveillance were so dishonorable and "nasty" that they were still not disclosed decades later.[77]

Radios were allowed in homes and dorms, but with so many transformers and electrical wires in Site Y's Tech Area, it was almost impossible to receive outside radio broadcasts. Attempting to partially fill this entertainment void, Los Alamos residents created their own radio station, known as the Community Radio Station or KRS, by October 1943. Most local residents listened regularly to KRS during its broadcast hours for an hour at noon and in the evenings. For security reasons, KRS was never licensed by the Federal Communications Commission; it transmitted such a weak signal that it could hardly be heard beyond Site Y's perimeter anyway. The small station featured classical music played from records borrowed from the scientists' private collections or played in person by the renowned physicist, Otto Frisch, introduced simply as "our pianist" for obvious security reasons. Robert Y. Porton, a KRS announcer, recalls that he was ordered never to use words like "Los Alamos" or "atomic" while on the air. In fact, intelligence officers regularly "reviewed the programming for classified information."[78] Few residents knew that the military had also built a radio intercept system to detect unauthorized transmissions, including an innocent ham radio that teenage boys set up in a tree house in the nearby woods.[79]

Financial transactions were kept under wraps as well. To prevent the tracing of new accounts in Santa Fe banks, scientists were instructed to bank by mail, using their pre-Los Alamos home banks. Hugh T. Richards thus opened a joint account with his mother in his hometown of DeRidder, Louisiana, just prior to moving to Los Alamos. Richards' and all civilian salaries were deposited directly to these home bank accounts. Meanwhile, with no banks or bank branches in Los Alamos, personal checks could only be cashed at a designated military office on The Hill. By 1945 the value of checks cashed in this manner equaled as much as four thousand dollars a day.[80] Josephine Julius, a WAC assigned to the check-cashing office, "had the [daily] thrill of having a car and guard take her to a particular bank in Santa Fe to exchange the checks for cash . . . . in the bank manager's office."[81]

Despite the dangerous nature of their work, scientists were not allowed to open new life insurance policies once they had moved to The Hill. Finding life or accident insurance coverage would have been difficult, if not impossible, in any case. Although Manhattan Project authorities attempted various solutions, "the problem of providing insurance was extremely complex and [was] never solved adequately," according to David Hawkins, Site Y's official historian.[82]

Filing income tax returns created another problem in security office efforts to conceal the scientists' whereabouts and duties.

Regardless of their actual training or responsibilities, all civilian scientists were instructed to complete their tax forms by listing their occupation as "engineer" and their employer as the Army Corps of Engineers. Code numbers were used instead of real names to further disguise the scientists' true identities.[83]

Other code numbers were used in lieu of real names on drivers' licenses, car registrations, gas rationing forms, and other official documents. If New Mexico police stopped a scientist on state or local highways, they would be shown a driver's license "of a nameless Engineer identified only as Number 185 [(in the case of Richard Feynman)], residing at Special List B, whose signature was, for some reason, Not Required."[84] And the odds of scientists being stopped by the police were good. As one lieutenant later acknowledged, "Some of the world's lousiest auto drivers developed the bomb."[85] Otto Frisch, for example, had his first accident the day after he received his nameless New Mexico drivers license.[86] Bernice Brode told an apocryphal story about a caravan of cars carrying "a group of Nobel Prize winners and deans of science, all traveling under false names." When the caravan was flagged down by a local police officer, each traveler politely refused to give his name. "'Tell that to the judge,'" retorted the policeman as he wrote out a summons, determined to teach the almighty Army a lesson." They were sorry, the scientists replied, but they could not appear before a judge either. All they could promise to do was to take the summons to higher military and civilian authorities. The befuddled policeman let them go.[87] To be less conspicuous and to avoid such awkward confrontations with the law, Deak Parsons went so far as to have his maroon Mercury painted dark green.[88]

Only one activity could not be arranged with coded numbers or by high level maneuvering. United States citizens at Site Y were effectively disenfranchised because a ballot box could not be placed in a town that did not appear on any map and enjoyed no official status. Only those who retained official residences in other states and had secured absentee ballots could vote in national elections, including the presidential election of 1944. As highly educated, often politically active citizens, their inability to vote caused considerable distress among the most vocal scientists and their wives. In a classic Catch-22, all Site Y residents were nevertheless required to pay New Mexico state income taxes, meaning that they were disenfranchised but were still expected to pay taxes on at least the state level.[89]

The only time residents could vote in Los Alamos was when a six-member Town Council was elected each six months, starting in August 1943. Scientists and their spouses used Town Council meetings to vent their many frustrations with living conditions and security regulations. Although the council had little real power, it helped to defuse at least some of the conflicts that plagued civil-military relations. The fact that Site Y had three post commanders in two and a half years (including Colonel John M. Harman, who was replaced in 1943 because he could not get along with several of the scientists, and Colonel Whitney Ashbridge, who was relieved of duty after suffering a heart attack in 1944) reflects the ongoing tension that characterized life on The Hill.[90]

Travel Restrictions

In another security precaution, travel was also strictly limited. Unless on official business or to handle personal emergencies, residents were not allowed to travel beyond Santa Fe. Once in Santa Fe, Site Y residents were to "maintain no social relations." They were definitely never to engage in "loose talk" using the forbidden terms or kinds of information banned from their private correspondence by Army censors.[91] Even casual encounters were to be reported to security personnel immediately. When Jane Wilson bumped into an old college friend on the streets of Santa Fe, it was "wonderfully exhilarating to see someone from the outside world," but she was so worried about saying anything about Site Y that "it was a relief to say goodbye." Comparing herself to "a child confessing that she had been naughty," Wilson dutifully reported her brief meeting to a security officer as soon as she returned home to Los Alamos.[92]

Living and working in Santa Fe daily, Dorothy McKibbin was especially aware of suspicious strangers lurking near her office or elsewhere in town. Years later she recalled that "Whenever a suspicious person showed up at [her] office . . . [she] had only to make a quick call and a G-2 [Army intelligence] agent would be on the trail of the suspect before he had left the plaza."[93]

In Santa Fe, scientists and their families often suspected that government agents were either trailing them or observing their actions from key vantage points. Their suspicions were often well-founded. Agents were ubiquitous. John Lansdale has acknowledged that the desk clerk at La Fonda, the busy Harvey House in Santa Fe, was in fact a government agent placed in an ideal position to monitor the comings and goings of all visitors. Waiters and bartenders were also agents at La Cantina (La Fonda's bar) and other popular eating and drinking establishments. Some scientists even suspected local gamblers and Native Americans who sold their arts and crafts on the Santa Fe plaza. Other agents were not as well disguised. Those in suits and felt hats were especially conspicuous among the informally attired general population of Santa Fe.[94] Just as they felt harassed by the censors who read their mail, scientists often felt resentment when shadowed in town. They couldn't go to Santa Fe, wrote Jane Wilson, "without being aware of hidden eyes upon [us], watching, waiting to pounce on that inevitable misstep."[95]

Rumors and the Press

Rumors about the purpose of Los Alamos soon spread in Santa Fe and surrounding communities. Reflecting the good-natured, live-and-let-live attitude of most New Mexicans of that time, local residents created facetious theories to explain the burst of new activity on the Pajarito Plateau. William McNulty of the *Santa Fe New*

Mexican kiddingly estimated that no less than 6,892 such rumors circulated during the war. Some said that Los Alamos had become a concentration camp built by Franklin Roosevelt's Democratic administration to house Republican opponents. Others insisted that it was an underground submarine base with headquarters below the surface at Ashley Pond in the center of Los Alamos. A third story claimed that Los Alamos was a home for pregnant WACs.[96]

But other stories heard by G-2 agents in Santa Fe came closer to the truth about Los Alamos' mission and worried Site Y leaders, including Robert Oppenheimer. To address these more valid rumors, Oppenheimer and security officers developed a counterespionage plan as early as April 1943. Meeting privately in his office, Oppenheimer asked two scientists and their wives if they would be willing to visit Santa Fe and spread a fabricated story about Los Alamos and its mission "to account for all the civilian scientists, for the supersecrecy, and for the loud booms that Santa Feans were beginning to hear" at all hours of the day. John and Priscilla Manley and Robert and Charlotte Serber were to let everyone in hearing range know that the government was making nothing less than an electric rocket up on The Hill.[97]

The Manley-Serber spy ring agreed to this assignment and proceeded to Santa Fe to visit the bar in La Fonda and at least one other drinking lounge. The foursome did its best to speak loudly in crowds and convincingly to individuals, but nothing seemed to work. In Charlotte Serber's words, "no ears cocked" and no one "showed . . . the slightest interest." When Robert Serber "practically took [a rancher] by his coat lapels" and announced his secret information, the cowman simply "grunted and ordered another drink." The counterespionage plan had clearly failed to sway or even slightly influence public opinion in the state capital.[98]

Despite this small setback, security officials remained determined to safeguard information about the bomb by establishing a gag rule on the press. Beginning in June 1943 and regularly thereafter, the Manhattan Project sent "confidential letters" to thousands of radio broadcasters, newspaper editors, reporters, and publishers forbidding them to disseminate any information regarding the "production or utilization of atom smashing, atomic energy, atomic fission, atomic splitting, or any of their equivalents." A long list of elements and their compounds, from uranium to ytterbium, were taboo as well.[99] By 1944 an army of government observers monitored 370 newspapers, seventy magazines, and countless radio stations to make sure that all censorship rules were obeyed. Even atomic energy-related articles published before the war were monitored, as when the publishers of the *Saturday Evening Post* were asked to report "at once" any requests for copies of a 1940 *Post* article on the atom by science reporter William L. Laurence. The *Post* replied that no such requests had ever been made.[100]

In New Mexico, the editor of the *Santa Fe New Mexican* told his reporters not to bother Dorothy McKibbin for stories about the whirlwind of activity that surrounded her downtown office.[101] When B.B. Dunne of the *New Mexican* vaguely mentioned that "there were a lot of scientists in town," he "got tangled in the ringer" by security officers.[102] On another occasion, a New York newspaper doing research for a feature story about Nobel Prize winners asked the *New Mexican* about one such scientist whose address was listed as Post Office Box 1663, Santa Fe. The *New Mexican* sent a letter to Box 1663 requesting an interview with the scientist, but received a most unexpected response: the following morning two security agents "jumped the cityroom" and made all sorts of accusations. After "a heap of protestations and avowals of innocence," it was agreed that the following telegram would be sent to New York: "Your man working for Mr. Whiskers [Uncle Sam] on extremely hush-hush project. No soap." The telegram was delivered in New York by a Western Union boy "flanked by a covey of guards."[103]

Other New Mexico newspapers experienced similar reactions. When the *Albuquerque Journal* reported that a forest fire in the Jemez Mountains had been extinguished with the help of Los Alamos personnel, "the editor was harshly reprimanded by security agents."[104] Newspaper editors and writers operated under what the *Santa Fe New Mexican* described as "probably the strictest censorship ever imposed upon the press of this state."[105] But the press' general cooperation was appreciated. At war's end, the *New Mexican* received a letter of commendation from General Groves, thanking the newspaper for helping to keep the Manhattan Project a secret so that the U.S. could enjoy the "element of surprise so vital to the application of the atomic bomb as a powerful weapon" against Japan.[106]

A Needed Respite: Edith Warner's Tearoom

Although travel away from Site Y was limited, the need to leave The Hill's strenuous work schedule and tight living conditions for even short periods was understood by everyone, including Robert Oppenheimer. As a result, the lab's director came to an informal agreement with Edith Warner, the owner of a small tearoom located about twelve miles east of Los Alamos near the bridge at Otowi Crossing. Warner and Tilano, her long-time companion from the San Ildefonso Pueblo, had operated their tearoom for several years, but with gasoline rationing and the closing of the Ranch School at Los Alamos, they had fewer and fewer customers during the war. To help the couple and otherwise provide a local destination for scientists in search of quiet dinners away from The Hill, Oppenheimer suggested that the tearoom be closed to all other customers and be exclusively available to four to five couples from Los Alamos several evenings a week. By December 1943 Warner wrote that she was "booked up weeks ahead." A year later she wrote, "I could serve every night and still have a waiting list." With security in mind, a "thoroughly undemocratic and mysterious process" determined the dates when grateful couples were allowed to travel to the tearoom to enjoy Warner's good home-cooked meals. Warner considered her efforts "a war job for me," although she was the first to admit that the scientists and their wives were "most interesting" and helped "solve my need for people."[107]

Bodyguards and Code Names

Manhattan Project scientists sent on long-distance missions faced much greater protection (or scrutiny). Personal bodyguards accompanied leading scientists like Oppenheimer, Edward Teller, Enrico Fermi, Deak Parsons, Arthur Compton, and Niels Bohr. According to one story, when Bohr absentmindedly crossed a New York street against a red light as many as six bodyguards jaywalked to keep up with him.[108] Most scientists nevertheless appreciated their guards largely because they had been selected not only for their security skills, but also because their personalities or interests matched those of the men they were assigned. Arthur Compton thus praised Julian Bernacchi, a law school graduate, a former member of the Chicago police force, and, like Compton, an avid baseball fan. According to Compton, "In any unusual situation Julian was always on guard [but he] knew how to disappear when there was obviously no need for his professional services." Compton added that "Julian was very useful to me in many ways, not the least of which was in making sure that I did not inadvertently neglect some of the many security precautions that I was expected to observe."[109] Most so-called bodyguards were, in fact, counterintelligence agents sent to watch scientists as much as to protect them. Rather than let Enrico Fermi "talk science" with just anyone, his Italian-speaking bodyguard "diverted Fermi's conversation to himself" whenever possible. Eventually, Fermi declared that John Baudino knew so much about the Manhattan Project from their conversations that "soon . . . he will need a bodyguard, too."[110] Most significantly, Andrew Walker's primary task as Robert Oppenheimer's "competent, able bodied, armed . . . chauffeur" was to keep him from driving alone "on any lonely road, such as the road from Los Alamos to Santa Fe" and "to keep an eye out for any untoward contacts by the physicist."[111] Round-the-clock military patrols also guarded

Oppenheimer's house in Los Alamos, requiring even Kitty Oppenheimer to show a pass when entering her own home on prestigious Bathtub Row.[112]

To further enhance secrecy in their travels, Oppenheimer and others were referred to by code names. Oppenheimer's code name was James Oberhelm, while Niel Bohr's was Nicolas Baker, Enrico Fermi's was Henry (or Eugene) Farmer, Edward Teller's was Ed Tilden, Hans Bethe's was Howard Battle, and James Chadwick's was James Chaffee. Arthur Holly Compton traveled so often that he was assigned several names: A.H. Comas, A.H. Comstock, A. Holly, and Mr. Black.[113]

Oppenheimer, Teller, Bethe, Fermi, and other top scientists were shadowed whenever they left the gates of Los Alamos. In the most famous incident of this kind, G-2 agents closely observed Oppenheimer's movements when he visited his former fiancee during a trip to the San Francisco Bay area in June 1943. Agents watched Oppenheimer and Jean Tatlock while they had drinks at the Top of the Mark, stayed the night at her apartment on Telegraph Hill, and drove to the airport together the next morning. Oppenheimer reportedly told Tatlock that he would not be able to see her for many months, was about to move to an undisclosed destination, and was unable to discuss the nature of his new work. Distraught, Jean Tatlock took her own life seven months later.[114]

Oppenheimer's plane trip to San Francisco was among his last during the war. Not trusting airline travel, General Groves insisted that Oppenheimer, Parsons, Compton, and other top scientists travel by train in an "enclosed Pullman space" whenever possible for safety and security reasons. Groves preferred railroad travel for himself as well. Wearing civilian clothes and carrying a pistol under his coat, he kept secret documents in his possession beneath his seat in Pullman compartments. All Manhattan Project officers were required to take the same precautions, using "specially designed pouches" for secret documents, carrying "not ostentatiously" visible weapons, and remaining sober at all times.[115]

High Fences and Military Guards

Back at Los Alamos, a 9'6" high wire-mesh fence topped with barbed wire strands surrounded the entire project. Stern warnings in *The Daily Bulletin* told residents that fences were "put in place for a purpose and the guards are authorized to keep people away from them. Don't make it necessary for the guard to use his weapon to keep you away. The guard means business when he orders you to halt."[116] If these warnings were not enough, Eleanor Jette remembered that the fence was "liberally festooned" with signs that read:

U.S. Government Property
DANGER! *PELIGRO!*
Keep out[117]

Sentries patrolled the exterior fence with orders to "prevent loitering and trespassing," inspect the condition of the fence, be alert to fires, and "report immediately suspicious persons or unusual occurrences to [the] Officer of the Day."[118]

The military police detachment (4817th Service Unit) assigned to patrol the fence and stand guard at all gates arrived in April 1943. Lawrence Antos, a young draftee from the Chicago area, and his fellow GIs were chosen for this critical duty based on their skills and their "unquestioned loyalty," as specified in a memo from Groves in February 1943.[119] Never told of their destination during their weeks of training at Fort Riley, Kansas, Antos recalls that he suspected that they were going to guard a Japanese-American internment camp somewhere out West. Instead, their services were so urgently needed to replace temporary civilian guards at Site Y that about fifty of them were sent ahead and the remaining fifty-three officers and men followed shortly thereafter.[120] By December 1943 their ranks had grown to 295. Eventually, the number of guards at Los Alamos equaled no fewer than nine officers and 486 enlisted men. Meanwhile, Site Y's Intelligence and Security Office staff expanded from just two officers to twenty-eight officers and seven civilians in the course of the war.[121]

Site Y's Technical Area was especially well patrolled by armed soldiers on horseback, on foot, and in radio-equipped vehicles. Half of all guards were posted inside the Tech Area during its early construction phase from May to December 1943. Thereafter, two perimeter foot patrols, gate guards, and a night fire guard kept close watch over Tech Area activities. Privates were posted for two hours on duty and four hours off, while noncommissioned officers worked six hours on and six hours off during each twenty-four hour duty period. One hundred and fifty-nine 1,500-watt flood lights lit the vicinity for those on guard. In addition, an RCA-manufactured prowler detector system was installed on the mesh-wire fence. Unusual mechanical vibrations on the fence produced audible and visual electrical signals to attract the attention of the sentry on duty, even indicating which sector of the fence had been disturbed.[122] When a new group of WACs hiked along the fence shortly after their arrival in mid-1943, "three MPs came thundering down the trail" on horseback. The unnerved WACs were ordered to "hike someplace else, and don't do this again."[123]

Badges, Burn Boxes, Locks, and Security Stamps

Color-coded badges were required to enter the three guarded entrances to the lab at various hours of the day and night. Scientists and officials with the highest level security clearance were issued white badges, meaning that they had access to all parts of the Tech Area at any time. Technicians and secretaries issued blue badges could only enter the shops and offices where they worked, while those with red or yellow badges were restricted to a limited number of lower security areas. Non-white badge holders could not enter the Tech Area between midnight and 6:00 A.M.[124]

Security guards, including at least one sergeant or corporal and four privates, inspected badges at the main Tech Area gate (#4) and at several check points within the lab. Other guards patrolled the halls, especially at night when all sensitive documents were to be locked in safes or, if no longer needed, deposited as "classified waste" in bright red "burn boxes."[125] Secretaries like Helen Embree burned everything left in burn boxes, accompanied by an MP to "witness the burning and to ensure that no pieces of paper slipped into one's pocket or escaped the incinerator without being retrieved and burned."[126] Guards also checked blackboards to make sure that all secret or revealing formulas had been erased by the end of each work day.[127]

While most scientists were scrupulous in following these procedures, others were not, much to the chagrin of those responsible for security. In one case, Hans Bethe absentmindedly left sensitive documents lying out when he went home for the day. To make an example of him, two MPs went to Bethe's house, woke him up, and insisted that he return to his lab to correct his mistake. "Everyone was more careful from then on," recalled Bernice Brode.[128]

Of course the most sensitive documents were handled with the utmost care. Documents were classified, in ascending order, as "confidential," "secret," and "top secret." Top secret documents were defined as those that revealed "production figures of end products peculiar to the [Manhattan] District," "critical information pertaining to the military use of the end products peculiar to the District," and information regarding intelligence (and counterintelligence) operations "which would imperil security agents."[129] Top secret documents were transmitted in double-sealed envelopes, clearly stamped "Top Secret," and labeled with the names of those who were to have access to the strictly guarded information enclosed. Top secret documents were also identified with serial numbers in an exacting record and filing system.[130] They were carefully stored in huge, three-combination vaults within the Tech Area; the imposing vault in Deak Parson's office was described as having "all the bearing and heft of a Sherman tank."[131] Only a limited number of specially cleared personnel had access to these vaults, with authority to allow or deny access to others. Mildred Tice, a WAC secretary for Site Y's legal counsel, controlled one such vault in her supervisor's office. She recalls the day that a scientist asked for a certain document in the vault for which he had not been cleared. When Tice refused to grant him access, he reportedly "banged on the table and shouted: 'Dammit, I wrote it!'"[132] Made impatient by such incidents, Leo Szilard at the Met Lab in Chicago spoke for scientists throughout the Manhattan Project when he later complained that "the most powerful weapon of this war was not the A-bomb, but the secrecy stamp."[133]

The Compartmentalization Feud

But while burn boxes, vaults, and secrecy stamps proved irksome for many, no restriction was potentially more bothersome to the scientists and their experimental work than a military policy recognized as completely alien to the creative scientific process: compartmentalization. According to military authorities led by Groves, it was absolutely necessary to divide scientists into four divisions (Theoretical, Experimental, Chemistry and Metallurgy, and Ordnance Engineering) that would work separately without knowing how other divisions were proceeding. Groves later wrote that

My rule was simple and not capable of misinterpretation— each man should know everything he needed to know to do his job and nothing else. Adherence to this rule not only provided an adequate measure of security, but it greatly improved over-all efficiency by making people stick to their knitting. And it made quite clear to all concerned that the project existed to produce a specific end product—not to enable individuals to satisfy their curiosity and to increase their scientific knowledge.[134]

"Compartmentalization of knowledge," declared Groves, "was the very heart of security."[135] "Groves was a tight man with a secret," according to one historian. "[He] never told anybody anything he didn't need to know, and sometimes balked at that."[136]

Predictably, most scientists at Los Alamos strenuously objected to General Groves' "need to know" policy as contrary to the scientific process and the free flow of ideas; only the rejected notion of making all scientists into officers seemed more alien to those accustomed to academic freedom and an open dialogue among colleagues. Edward U. Condon was so shocked by Groves' planned compartmentalization that he "could hardly believe my ears." Convinced that such a policy would make an "extremely difficult job" much harder, Condon told Oppenheimer that it would be like trying to work with "three hands tied behind your back." Frustrated, Condon resigned from the Manhattan Project and returned to his former position at the Westinghouse Research Labs as early as April 1943.[137]

In a rare moment of friction between Groves and his director at Los Alamos, Oppenheimer argued in favor of a far more open system of information sharing. Oppenheimer and others favored the creation of a weekly colloquium at which all scientists with white badge security clearance would gather to share new developments in their respective divisions and on the atomic weapon as a whole. As John Lansdale later explained, "Oppie [(the director's nickname)] thought that to effectively and rapidly complete the project, work should proceed as a single project with each scientist being fully familiar with what the others were doing."[138] Colloquia were also held to develop an esprit de corps, "a sense of common effort and cause, with younger men acting as equals to their seniors in the contributing of ideas or criticism."[139] Oppenheimer further argued that "Giving the scientific staff adequate information . . . would actually enhance security, for the scientists would a achieve a better understanding of the necessity for secrecy."[140]

Despite his strong initial opposition, General Groves reluctantly conceded to the scientific need (if not the security wisdom) of holding colloquia at Site Y. Los Alamos' first colloquium met on May 30, 1943, in a heavily-guarded venue (Theater #2) large enough to seat all participants, albeit outside the Tech Area's gates.[141] However, to reenforce the urgent need for tight security, Groves and his fellow officers requested that President Roosevelt himself write a letter to Oppenheimer not only to encourage the vital work at Site Y, but also to stress that the "outcome of your labors is of such great significance to the nation" that it must remain a "secret among secrets." The president added his "deep appreciation of [the scientists'] willingness to undertake the tasks which lie before [you] in spite of the possible dangers and personal sacrifices involved."[142] Oppenheimer dutifully read the president's letter of June 29, 1943, to his fellow scientists at a colloquium session in early July.

Unable to suppress colloquia within Site Y, Groves attempted to prevent a similar flow of information between Los Alamos and other Manhattan Project sites.[143] Leo Szilard, a major critic of the latter policy and of General Groves' policies overall, claimed that such compartmentalization between sites "held up the project by as much as eighteen months."[144]

A Safe Secret in Theory

With constant vigilance, Site Y was considered the most guarded, most secretive military or civilian installation in the United States during World War II. Security clearances, censorship, fences, passes, badges, locks, burn boxes, and security stamps were all designed to assure American leaders that the secret of the atomic bomb was as safe as humanly possible in Los Alamos. After all, not even the vice president of the United States knew of the Manhattan Project, no less its intended purpose in the war. This was, at least, the theory.

2
PRACTICE

"I thought then and later events . . . proved that [maintaining a secret,] insulated city in the middle of a desert is more easily postulated in theory than it is carried out in actual practice."

John Lansdale
April 16, 1954[1]

These, then, were the main security rules that scientists, their dependents, and military personnel were expected to respect and obey during their years of service at Los Alamos. But how were these seemingly strict rules of behavior carried out? And how were they enforced? Surely, those who defied the rules and compromised Site Y's security would face clearly understood, harsh penalties, both personally and professionally. As Lieutenant Myrtle C. Bachelder later recalled, "[Peer] de Silva told me, essentially, to button my lip about the place and promised dire consequences if I didn't."[2] Rumors circulated in military and civilian circles as to just what these "dire consequences" might include.

Security Breaches and Dubious Punishment
In the course of the Manhattan Project's existence, the Army's Counter-Intelligence Corps (CIC) investigated over three hundred "probable" espionage and sabotage cases. Three investigations led

to tough penalties for the scientists involved. In separate, unrelated cases, surveillance teams observed Joseph W. Weinberg in California and Clarence Hiskey of the Metallurgical Lab in Chicago as they met with known Soviet agents or spies. In both cases, the scientists lost their security clearances, were soon drafted into the Army, and were dispatched to bases in Alaska where the odds of enemy capture and interrogation were almost as remote as the bases themselves. General Groves was said to have so much evidence that a third scientist was passing secrets to the Soviets that Groves insisted that he be drafted and sent off to basic training. Each time a company he was assigned to would complete its basic training and be shipped out, the accused would be kept behind to repeat the rigors of boot camp over and over again.[3]

It would seem that this form of punishment would be more than adequate to deter additional attempts to compromise security. But this was not always the case. The penalty of being drafted and then exiled to either the Aleutian Islands or a perennial boot camp could only work to deter young scientists of military service age. Older scientists might dread the career-ending loss of their security clearance, but there is no record of any senior scientists losing their clearance during the war. As will be seen, only one scientist was asked to leave Site Y, but, as an emigre, he simply returned to his native Poland, having already planned to leave the Manhattan Project. Moreover, what punishment existed was hardly well publicized and hardly a deterrent, if punishment was in fact a deterrent to such transgressions. The fate of an unfortunate few was rumored, but never officially confirmed. "[H]ad anybody been caught and publicly punished," write two recent observers, "Manhattan Project personnel might have better understood both the threat and the need for security."[4]

Realities of Censorship

Problems in enforcing security regulations went far beyond the correlation of crime and punishment. Every aspect of Site Y's security system could be—and often was—compromised. This was certainly true of censorship regulations. As Colonel Lansdale later testified before a post-war Atomic Energy Commission hearing, mail was censored, but "on a spot check basis." Only the mail of the "more important scientists and those upon whom we had derogatory information" was censored "one hundred percent" of the time.[5] Thus when Louis Jacot wrote a letter that mentioned a mountain near Los Alamos, a censor returned it to him. But when Jacot resent the letter without deleting the objectionable information, it left Site Y without further interference. A lack of available Army censors and the sheer volume of mail prohibited a more thorough operation, although censor markings appeared on all mail to give the appearance that every piece of correspondence had been scrutinized.[6]

Richard Feynman chafed at the rules and had so many run-ins with the censors assigned to Site Y that he became an expert on what would or would not pass by their well-trained, skeptical eyes. In fact, scientists began coming to Feynman for advice whenever they wrote letters they hoped would not be delayed or changed by the censors. Feynman even took bets that he could beat the censors at their own game.[7] Clearly, if individuals like Feynman could outwit the censors, coded messages might well have been sent, especially by those whose mail was not subjected to censorship one hundred percent of the time. Even more likely, those who truly wanted to evade the censors with top secret information simply had to break the rule about using mail drops in Los Alamos. Mail could easily be sent via censor-free mail boxes in Santa Fe or in other nearby communities by those with the treasonous will to do so.

The censorship of newspapers, magazines, and radio stations proved to be equally untenable with time. Sending out hundreds of "confidential letters" to regularly remind the press not to mention atomic research was, in fact, a frequent reminder that something controversial involving atomic energy was going on. Not every editor, reporter, and radio announcer could be trusted not to share this basic information with others, if only in passing. And private slips could start curious foreign agents on the trail to the ultimate purpose of Site Y and the Manhattan Project as a whole.[8]

A rash of censorship violations occurred in late 1943. Newspapers like the *Washington Post* and the *Spokane Spokesman-Review* ran stories that referred to possible Congressional investigations of military spending on secret research projects. Quick action by government agents "led to withdrawal of the articles before they received wide circulation."[9] A later article speculated on the sudden, hurried activity in Los Alamos. Lacking photographs, the *Cleveland Plain Dealer* featured a political cartoon depicting "guards in . . . battle helmets . . . with bulldog faces."[10] Other security breaks leaked information about the Manhattan Project via a 1944 national radio broadcast and a February 1945 article in *Business Week* about the Hanford, Washington, phase of the project.[11] Finally, when the government's War Manpower Commission advertised for much-needed personnel at Hanford and indirectly revealed the importance of the work involved, the Associated Press picked up the story and sent it by wire all over the nation. The incident "precipitated general rebellion among newspaper editors who had been held to secrecy in part by [Manhattan] District promises that no one else would 'scoop' them."[12]

Not even threats by Groves' security men could dam the dike once it had begun to leak. Although many editors continued to respect the gag order on news from Los Alamos, enough information became available to ultimately compromise Site Y's location and probable purpose. In the words of a recent historian, "Groves' campaign for complete silence outside the [Manhattan Project's] fences had failed."[13]

Easy Entry

Rules regarding passes to be shown when entering or leaving Los Alamos were compromised with relative ease. In the first months of Site Y's operation, passes were no more than typed notes signed by Oppenheimer and three designated officers on ordinary stationary inspected by locally-recruited, poorly trained civilian guards at the front gate. According to an early resident, this primitive system "resulted in writer's cramp for the Director, bad tempers for the typists, and after a few days of use, a collection of the most bedraggled passes ever presented at an Army Post."[14] Charlotte Serber could have mentioned that this use of typed passes was also dangerous to the project in its early development because passes could be easily typed and forged by any number of unapproved outsiders.

There are seemingly countless anecdotes of scientists, their family members, and even Army personnel misplacing or forgetting their passes, but evading the guards on duty at the main gate into Site Y. Edward F. Hammel recalls the evening that he and his wife were driving with friends back to Los Alamos when Hammel's wife realized that she had forgotten her pass. "Upon arriving at the Main Gate . . . she fortunately had with her an unopened package of cigarettes (with the cellophane wrapper still intact around them)." Hammel writes that from the back seat of the car she "quickly and quite calmly flashed [the cigarette box] in front of the MP's flashlight and we were all waved through without incident."[15]

Short of improvising with cigarette boxes, residents could easily stowaway in cars driven by friends or relatives. Teenagers frequently used this method when their parents had punished them by confiscating their passes in hopes of confining them to The Hill. In daylight hours, stowaways were usually transported in car trunks until they passed the gate and could be let out to continue their trips as regular passengers. When seven-year-old Claudio Segre forgot his pass on a Sunday outing with his parents and the Fermis, Emilio Segre smuggled his son past Gate #1 in the trunk of his car rather than go back home for the missing ID. Pretending that he was on a secret government mission, Claudio hardly minded the brief imposition.[16] At night, those without passes lay covered by blankets on the floor of their escape vehicle until they passed the gate and could surface from their hiding places. These practices were so common, and car searches were so infrequent, that even soldiers who guarded the main gate were known to travel by trunk if they lacked authorized leaves to go into town. Even large equipment could be transported without detection. Joseph Hirschfelder recalls an instance when a technician was bold enough to unscrew a turret lathe from the floor of his shop in the lab, use a portable crane to load it in the bed of an Army truck, cover it with a tarpaulin, and drive past two gate guards without inspection. The thief proceeded to Santa Fe and attempted to sell his cargo to a man he had met at the bar in La Fonda. The technician might have succeeded in his caper if he had not chosen a potential buyer who happened to be an undercover agent. The thief was promptly arrested.[17]

It became so simple to enter or leave Site Y that mathematician John von Neumann bet intelligence chief Peer de Silva that he could smuggle a fellow scientist into Los Alamos. De Silva first took the bet, but soon changed his mind for fear that von Neumann might be successful, causing great embarrassment to de Silva and his entire security staff.[18]

As early as June 1943 Oppenheimer informed Groves that "several thousand essentially uncleared people [have] access to the post."[19] By October 1943 a security report declared that "The post is easily entered by unauthorized persons." In addition to scientists and their families, hundreds of local workers came and went each day as they labored to transport coal and supplies, construct new buildings, and serve as domestic help. The 1943 report concluded that "It has been actually demonstrated . . . that a person without any kind of a badge or pass can easily come from outside Los Alamos not only into the post but into the technical area itself."[20] If little Ellen Bradbury was unable to enter Los Alamos to seek medical attention, it was because her family did not yet live in Los Alamos and had not yet learned how to evade the guards with methods that were common knowledge to all but the most scrupulous (or naive) residents of The Hill.

Porous Fences

Intruders had little more difficulty penetrating Site Y's exterior fence. Not wanting to be inconvenienced by having to go around to the main gate, many residents simply dug holes under the fence in order to exit or enter. Digging holes took no special tools or skills. In fact, it was so easy that children regularly dug holes to crawl under the fence and play in the surrounding canyons and woods. The guards' patrol became so regular and predicable that children learned it quickly and knew when it was safe to come and go without interference. Eric and Eleanor Jettes' son, Bill, was one of many children who were known to enter and leave "at will." Children became so adept at this feat that they sometimes served as guides for adults who sought the same easy access to the world beyond their fence.[21]

Richard Feynman explored nearly the entire length of Los Alamos' exterior fence, finding many exit holes with "well-beaten paths" leading to them. To prove that the holes existed—and to cause some additional mischief—Feynman flustered the guards on duty by crawling under the fence and walking back through the main gate, conspicuously displaying his pass as he entered. Moments later he retraced his route, mystifying the guard who "couldn't understand how a man could keep coming in and never going out."[22]

Feynman reported his discovered escape routes to security officers, but received an uninterested response. Feynman suspected those in charge wanted to allow access by residents of nearby pueblos who frequented Site Y's inexpensive movie theaters and post exchange. Some believed that Oppenheimer himself knew of this practice and condoned it. More prudish minds suspected that soldiers allowed prostitutes to enter as well.[23]

Larger holes in the fence, rather than under it, were created when cattle broke through and when horseback riders like Eleanor

Jette "went prepared to take the fence down and replace it when we returned."[24] Mounted patrols were seldom effective in guarding the long exterior barrier. In fact, scenes of soldiers "thundering down the trail" on horseback to frighten those who walked along the fence were rare. Indeed, at least one former guard recalls that the use of mounted patrols was eventually abandoned because, among other reasons, guards were known to fall asleep in their saddles. Their obliging horses returned to Site Y's stables where the sleeping riders would eventually be found and woken up.[25] If children, resident adults, and local Native Americans could casually learn the schedule of mounted and foot patrols and come and go at will, how much more accessible was Los Alamos to highly trained agents dispatched on missions to enter and cause serious mischief in the area?

The Tech Area's perimeter was far better protected, but even it had its share of problems. The prowler detector fence was, in fact, too sensitive, registering the least vibration, such as a strong wind, and causing "more trouble than good." The system was not used after January 1945 and was entirely removed in May of that year.[26]

Although not part of the exterior fence, a single outside electrical wire caused additional problems when a "suicidal" bird perched on it "in such a way as to short the electrical system," proving that a human saboteur could do similar harm. Groves later recalled that "We had to shut down an entire building . . . and it was several days before operations again became normal."[27]

Problems in the Technical Area

And what about security within the lab itself? Did color-coded badges, interior patrols, burn boxes, and safes create the strict security that officers like Groves and de Silva attempted to enforce? Did isolated incidents like bringing Hans Bethe back to his office in the dark of night to lock classified documents make a difference in improved security, as Bernice Rode and others believed? Unfortunately, as with nearly every other aspect of security at Los Alamos, these efforts produced only limited positive results.

As early as the summer of 1943 a memo to all group leaders at Site Y reported as many as three to six serious breaches of security in the lab each day. Typical infractions included scientists taking books and documents home, not burning "classified waste," and leaving classified documents lying about, unsecured at night. Conditions hardly improved with time. By the fall of 1944 nightly patrols confiscated an average of thirty documents a week.[28]

Although the Tech Area was supposed to close down at the end of each work day, many dedicated scientists and staff members worked far into the evening and sometimes through the night. To gain access to materials in normally locked cabinets after hours, scientists were known to open padlocks by simply sawing their shackles close to the bodies of impeding locks. After using what they so urgently needed, these same scientists replaced the padlocks with their broken shackles realigned, making it appear that the locks were secure when they actually were not.[29]

Predictably, Richard Feynman recognized locks as another opportunity to prove that security at Los Alamos was woefully insufficient. But rather than simply saw off padlocks, Feynman focused on cracking combination locks found on file cabinets and safes holding top secret documents essential to the Manhattan Project's success. Taking up to a year and a half to perfect his skill (and self-confessed obsession), Feynman eventually became so well known for his safecracking ability that colleagues and, to his glee, officers often called on him to open locks when they had forgotten combinations or, worse, impatiently sought access to file cabinets or safes in other offices rather than wait for those responsible for these combinations to return.[30]

Feynman discovered that there was seldom anything mysterious about the combination of most locks at Site Y. About one out of every five locks in his building used one of two simple combinations that came with the locks from the factory where they were manufactured: 25-0-25 or 50-25-50. Most other combinations were set to obvious numbers having to do with math or science (such as the value of pi reversed) or the scientists' personal lives (such as a family member's birthday). Using these and other well-practiced methods, Feynman could open a lock in as little as a few minutes or as long as eight hours, with an average of four hours per safe. As part of his fun, the amateur safecracker often embarrassed his colleagues "either by leaving their safes open so that they were scolded by the security officer, or by leaving mysterious messages inside" and signing them with names like "Wise Guy." The only safe that Feynman could never crack was actually a solid concrete room with a large wheel lock like those found on safe-deposit vaults. According to Feynman, his inability to solve this last great mystery was more from lack of time and access than necessarily from lack of skill.[31] Feynman nevertheless made his point on most locks: if he could open them so could less loyal hands. Unfortunately, little was done to change the locks or alter the combinations and thereby improve security at Site Y.

Major Breakdown #1: Security Clearances

But security problems involving censored letters, gate passes, exterior fences, and locks represented only the tip of a larger mass of problems at Los Alamos during the war. Troubles in three other areas—security clearances, information access, and travel—were far more serious, amounting to three major breakdowns in security at Site Y. These were, in fact, the flaws in security that finally led to as many as six serious security leaks from Site Y. Not even Richard Feynman appreciated the depth and extent of the problems that surfaced as work progressed and the time to test the atomic bomb drew near.

At first, security clearances seemed thorough and exacting to the point of annoyance. But keeping up with the demand for security clearances grew more and more difficult. The trouble stemmed from Los Alamos' rampant population growth. Originally

Oppenheimer had estimated that he would need an elite group of perhaps thirty scientists and an equally small support staff to create an atomic bomb within about a year. Even by July 1943 Oppenheimer believed that seventy scientists and sixty support staff could do the job.[32]

But, faced with the true magnitude and complexity of the task before them, population figures grew much faster than anyone had anticipated. By the end of 1943 there were about five hundred scientists and support staff. By the end of 1944 the number equaled about 1,700, and in mid-1945 it had climbed to close to 2,500. In one month alone (in late 1944), 190 new machinists and toolmakers were quickly recruited and sent to Site Y.[33] Adding dependents, military personnel, and others, the total population of Los Alamos had skyrocketed to about six thousand by the time of the Trinity Site test in July 1945.[34] In the words of Site Y's official historian, the population "doubled, tripled, [and] quadrupled before anyone could figure out what was happening. . . . It always grew much faster than anyone could anticipate."[35] At least one scientist claimed that Oppenheimer's low estimate of how many men and women would be needed to invent and complete the "gadget" was "Oppie's worst error."[36]

Each of Los Alamos' thousands of residents had to be cleared as an acceptable security risk. While low-level security clearances were not difficult, higher level clearances for higher level scientists were much more complex and time consuming. Those assigned to security clearance operations simply could not keep up with the steadily increasing backlog. As Colonel Lansdale later admitted, "we stretched our clearance procedure when the pressure was on for personnel."[37] As a result, many scientists and support staff members, including Oppenheimer himself, were recruited, sent to Los Alamos, and were at work in the lab before their security checks had been completed, no less approved.[38]

Final security reports on those already in Los Alamos were sometimes less than satisfactory. According to Lieutenant Colonel

Kenneth D. Nichols of Groves' Manhattan Project staff, "Sometimes the final determination of personal [sic] security clearance would rest on the importance of the contribution the person was making" rather than on "the damaging information disclosed in his security file."[39] In the case of David Hawkins, for example, the subject had had clear leftist connections in his past, but was a close associate of Oppenheimer's and, later, the project's official historian. Despite the concern of security officers, Hawkins continued to enjoy Oppenheimer's "great confidence," knew most secret information, and served as one of the three members of the highly sensitive Lab Security Committee that determined who could attend weekly colloquium sessions, among other important duties.[40]

Seen from a different angle, the rapid increase in Los Alamos' wartime population prevented the building of a counterintelligence network within the Manhattan Project overall and at Site Y in particular. According to Soviet spymaster Pavel Sudoplatov,

> From an intelligence point of view the FBI's failure to detect [Soviet] espionage rings is understandable. The personnel in the Manhattan Project were assembled hastily and . . . . [t]here was no time for the FBI during the year and a half it took to organize the Manhattan Project to establish a strong counterintelligence network of agent informers among the scientific personnel of the project. That was absolutely necessary for detection of mole penetration.[41]

And what was true of the FBI was equally true of Groves' counterintelligence efforts. Without its own spies within the Manhattan Project to identify possible spies at work for the Soviets, Site Y's security system could be easily compromised.

General Groves clearly put progress on the bomb ahead of security when he approved a system to expedite Los Alamos' cumbersome security clearance process. In the interest of time, Groves allowed Oppenheimer to vouch for the loyalty of top-ranking scientists urgently needed at Site Y. Statements from three laboratory employees were all that was needed to clear junior scientists and technicians. Other employees were simply vouched for by their immediate supervisors.[42] In other words, security clearances were often left in the hands of security amateurs who knew and appreciated the urgent need for additional scientific help far more than they knew and appreciated the need for tight security and utmost loyalty. It is little wonder that Oppenheimer referred to this vouching procedure as "the 'two-bit' clearance" when it was used before Site Y was ever built.[43] Well aware of the great risks involved in clearing so many men and women under pressure, Groves candidly wrote in his memoirs that "The possibility of betrayal . . . became directly proportionate to the number of people employed" at Los Alamos.[44]

The Controversy Over Oppenheimer

The most controversial security clearance of the entire Manhattan Project (and perhaps the war) involved J. Robert Oppenheimer himself. Oppenheimer had been born into an affluent German business family in 1904. He was raised in New York City, earned his undergraduate degree at Harvard in three years (class of 1925), studied at Cambridge University, and received his doctoral degree in physics at the University of Gottingen in 1927. Returning to the United States from Europe in 1929, he accepted concurrent academic appointments at the University of California in Berkeley and the California Institute of Technology in Pasadena. Oppenheimer soon achieved legendary status at Berkeley "where devoted students assured standing-room-only status for his witty, dense, and scintillating lectures on modern theoretical physics."[45] Absorbed by his study of physics and his reading of great literature, Oppenheimer was, in his words, "almost wholly divorced from the contemporary [political and economic] scene" of the late 1920s and early 1930s.[46]

For better or worse, Oppenheimer's political isolation began to crumble in 1936 when he began to see the impact of the Great Depression on his students and began to experience a "smoldering fury about the [Nazis'] treatment of Jews in Germany," where several of his relatives still lived.[47] Politically naive, the young scientist became interested in leftist ideology through his relationship with Jean Tatlock, her "leftwing friends," and his younger brother Frank. Claiming that he read but never accepted Communist dogma, Oppenheimer nevertheless supported various Communist causes and fervently backed the Loyalist movement in the Spanish Civil War. He generously contributed to or joined "just about" every Communist front organization on the West Coast.[48]

Oppenheimer described his ties to Communist groups as "very brief and very intense"; his interest in them evaporated by the early 1940s almost as quickly as it had developed in the mid-1930s.[49] He became disillusioned with the Soviet Union and its ideology when Joseph Stalin concluded the Nazi-Soviet pact of 1939 and committed clear acts of military aggression against both Poland and Finland. Meeting Kitty Harrison, his future wife and a disillusioned former member of the Communist Party, eliminated whatever interest Oppenheimer still had in organizations like the American Association of Scientific Workers, the California Consumers Union, and the California Teachers Union.[50]

General Groves first met Robert Oppenheimer at a luncheon hosted by the president of the University of California on October 8, 1942. Having been assigned to oversee the Manhattan Project as recently as September 23, Groves did not take long to decide that a separate research facility was needed and that Oppenheimer was the right person for the highly sensitive job of leading it. The general was especially impressed by Oppenheimer's breadth of knowledge and ability to explain abstract concepts in basic terms. As a professional engineer, not a scientist, Groves needed a director who could explain the intricacies of theoretical and experimental physics in words the general could understand and act on with confidence.[51] Groves was also impressed that, unlike most scientists he had met, Oppenheimer's "obvious brilliance was offset by a surprising lack of pretention."[52] Oppenheimer's lack of a Nobel Prize or experience as the chair of a major physics department or lab may have placed him on the second tier of scientists in the academic world, but it undoubtedly made Groves feel more comfortable and at ease. Although the two men came from vastly different worlds, they somehow "cooperated beautifully" from the start. Ideally for Groves, he could rely on Oppenheimer to deal with the unruly scientists the general never could comprehend, no less manage directly. Ideally for Oppenheimer, he could exploit the scientists' mistrust of Groves to unite them and manage them more easily.[53]

But Oppenheimer's appointment as the director of Site Y ran into major problems with military officials and civilian leaders other than General Groves. Although Oppenheimer had severed his ties to all Communist organizations by 1942, skeptics in the FBI and military expressed deep concern about his past affiliations and on-going friendships with known Communists still under investigation. The FBI "loudly insisted" that Groves review the "lengthy and elaborate" file its agents had compiled on the Berkeley physicist.[54] In addition, Lieutenant Colonel Boris T. Pash, Groves' top security officer in the San Francisco area, remained convinced that Oppenheimer was a Communist sympathizer. Among other evidence, Pash, a White Russian refugee who "roundly hated all things Communist," used Oppenheimer's surreptitious rendezvous with his former lover, Communist Jean Tatlock, as proof of Oppenheimer's questionable loyalty. Pash also fretted about Oppenheimer's contacts with other suspected Communists, including several of his former students and colleagues at Berkeley. The colonel felt that any of these associates could persuade or even blackmail Oppenheimer into sharing secret information with the Soviets. In an urgent letter to John Lansdale, Pash argued that Groves' choice as the scientific director of Los Alamos should be "removed completely from the Project and dismissed from employment by the United States government."[55]

But nothing could change Groves' mind. Acting on a pure

hunch, Groves overruled all the advice he had been given by his own men and outside security agencies. Despite his deep aversion to Communism and belief that anyone with any connection to Communist groups was "not only unpatriotic but also showed very poor judgement and questionable intelligence,"[56] Groves approved Oppenheimer's clearance on July 20, 1943, writing to the District Engineer that

> In accordance with my verbal directions of July 15, it is desired that clearance be issued for the employment of Julius Robert Oppenheimer without delay, irrespective of the information which you have concerning Mr. Oppenheimer. He is absolutely essential to the project.[57]

But some still doubted Robert Oppenheimer's trustworthiness. When Lieutenant Colonel Nichols notified Oppenheimer of the general's unilateral action to approve his clearance, Nichols advised the scientist that "In the future, please avoid seeing your questionable friends, and remember, whenever you leave Los Alamos, we will be tailing you."[58]

Perhaps remembering this advice, and otherwise concerned with security himself, Oppenheimer asked to meet with Lieutenant Colonel Pash and Lieutenant Lyall Johnson of the Manhattan Project's security office just over a month after the scientist's mandated clearance by Groves. Oppenheimer reported that he and three other scientists had been contacted by the Soviet consulate in San Francisco by way of "other people, who were troubled by [the contacts], and sometimes came and discussed them with me."[59] Pressed to divulge who these "other people" might be, Oppenheimer refused. Oppenheimer refused again when he was asked while traveling by train with General Groves and Colonel Lansdale on a project-related trip from Wyoming to Chicago; he explained that he simply wanted to protect an innocent man. A few days later, on September 12, Lansdale questioned Oppenheimer a third time at an office in the Pentagon in Washington, D.C. Their session lasted nearly two hours, and, while

Oppenheimer was quite willing to offer the names of other suspected "Reds," he still would not identify the individual who had contacted him nine months earlier. Finally, on December 12, 1943, Groves himself confronted Oppenheimer at the conclusion of one of the general's several tours of the lab at Los Alamos. Traveling alone with Groves down the winding road to Santa Fe, Oppenheimer at last revealed the name that he had held back for so long: Haakron Chevalier, a personal friend and a fellow faculty member at Berkeley.[60]

But the "Chevalier incident," as it was forever known, did not end on the road to Santa Fe that cold winter evening. Indeed, it would haunt Oppenheimer throughout the war and long after, less because he had taken so long to name Chevalier than because he had lied about other scientists being contacted by the Soviet consulate via Chevalier. Whatever small amount of trust security agents had had in Oppenheimer had been further reduced, if not eliminated. A month after Oppenheimer's "confession" to Groves, Peer de Silva telegraphed Lansdale from Los Alamos that Oppenheimer could not be trusted because "His loyalty to the Nation is divided."[61] Pash was even more emphatic in his estimation of Oppenheimer in the aftermath of the director's revelation, declaring that "J.R. Oppenheimer is playing a key part in the attempts of the Soviet Union to secure, by way of espionage, highly secret information which is vital to the security of the United States."[62]

Despite these statements by his own staff, Groves never wavered in his opinion of Oppenheimer either because he remained convinced that the physicist was the right man for the job at Los Alamos or because, as some have suspected, he wanted to use the issue of Oppenheimer's loyalty as a form of leverage in dealing with Oppenheimer, in dealing with Site Y's scientists through Oppenheimer, or to secure Oppenheimer's support on controversial bomb-related policy questions. Oppenheimer's past, like a sword of Damocles, hung over his head with "only the hand of General Groves preventing it from descending" to end his work in the Manhattan

Project and preclude his significant role in history.[63]

Regardless of the reason for his clearance approval, Oppenheimer's celebrated case served as a prime example of the problems caused by Los Alamos' "two-bit" voucher security clearance system. If anyone is to be praised or blamed for Robert Oppenheimer's security clearance during World War II, it is Leslie Groves who not only cleared Oppenheimer originally, but continued to support him throughout the war.[64]

The British Mission and Niels Bohr

The U.S. government had adequate information to question Robert Oppenheimer's loyalty. However, it was far more difficult to obtain adequate information to make sound security decisions regarding foreign scientists recruited to share their expertise at Los Alamos. Often refugees from fascist countries in Europe, these scientists were generally considered good security risks; as Groves wrote, "it seemed highly probable that they could be entrusted." But Groves was the first to admit that "it was always possible that someone with disloyal intentions might slip through our screening procedures."[65]

The odds of someone with "disloyal intentions" slipping into Los Alamos increased greatly with the arrival of the British Mission. The mission, consisting of twenty-two top-level scientists, had been recruited to assist in the making of the bomb at Site Y after December 1943. Based on a diplomatic agreement between the United States and its ally Great Britain, Groves was "forced to allow the British to do their own security checking on their own scientists."[66] British security clearance methods were even more cursory than the Americans', especially when checking on the German and Italian emigres in their ranks. Groves claimed to have done additional checking on "those whose records of prior affiliations were not available to us or to the British Government," but, if he did so, it was done either very quickly or very poorly, as later events were to prove.[67]

Groves was soon aware that his security clearance system

had not adequately screened out all scientists and military personnel of questionable trustworthiness and loyalty. Realizing that foxes had already entered his supposedly safe hen house, Groves had limited options on how to respond. As he later explained, by the time a disloyal individual would have been identified, he probably would have acquired valuable information and

> To remove him would create only a greater hazard, particularly if he thought our suspicion of him unjustified. (I remembered that Benedict Arnold's treason had been sparked by his feeling that he had been unfairly treated.) Moreover, if we were to dismiss a person without publicizing the proof, which we would not want to do, the understandable resentment of his friends and associates in the project might seriously interfere with their work.[68]

Trials of suspected civilian spies or the courts-martial of military personnel were out of the question given the publicity that would undoubtedly accompany such proceedings.[69] These circumstances help to explain why even the few cases that led to punishment at Los Alamos were not well publicized to serve as a deterrent to others. In Groves' studied opinion, when scientists were suspected of subversive acts they were usually "retained in the belief that from a security standpoint it was safer to keep them [where they could be watched] than it was to let them go."[70]

In at least one high-profile case, a top foreign scientist was recruited to Los Alamos and retained not only because his brilliant mind and skills were needed, but also so he could be watched more closely and prevented from speaking out of hand, as he was known to do. Security officers, led by Groves, seldom thought of Niels Bohr as a potential Communist spy, but they did consider him "a loose cannon, too eminent to discipline, [but] impossible to ignore."[71] After Bohr barely escaped capture by the Nazis in his native Denmark, he was "treated less as a man than as an extraordinarily vulnerable secret which must on no account fall into enemy [hands]."[72] As a result, when Bohr was flown to London over the North Sea, he was assigned a seat "just over the bomb bay, so that by turning a handle he could be dropped into the sea . . . in the case of a German attack."[73] No attack occurred. Later, when Bohr and his son were flown to New York, they were accompanied by two British detectives who were joined by two Manhattan Project secret agents and two FBI officers when the Bohrs landed in the United States. Not trusting Bohr to travel across the United States to Los Alamos alone, General Groves and Richard Tolman of the National Defense Research Committee accompanied the Dutch genius by train. Groves reportedly lectured Bohr for twelve hours "on what he was and was not to say henceforth." Although Bohr kept nodding to everything the general said en route to New Mexico, Groves discovered that the scientist "was saying everything he promised he would not" within five minutes after their arrival.[74] Given his propensity to talk, the secret to the atomic bomb was considered far safer with Niels Bohr "exiled for the duration at Site Y."[75]

Major Breakdown #2: Information Access

Many who received rather easy clearance (or were identified as security risks but were allowed to stay) had regular access to top secret information about activities on The Hill. Most could have broken into Tech Area files and safes (as Feynman proved was possible), but there was no need. They simply had to attend the weekly Tuesday night colloquium meetings held at Theater #2 to learn the progress of Site Y's individual divisions as well as the bomb overall. Scientists who arrived after the colloquium began in May 1943 were hardly at a disadvantage: they were provided with a twenty-four-page mimeographed booklet called "The Los Alamos Primer," written to "bring scientists up to speed on the theory of [atomic] bomb making" so they could join in and contribute to the exchange of ideas at all future weekly sessions.[76]

Although only white badge scientists were authorized to attend colloquium meetings, scientists and technicians with lesser security clearances could gain entry with the permission of a credentials committee or, if turned down by the committee, by Oppenheimer himself. But not even attendance at these meetings was necessary to learn information when scientists were ready to share what they had learned with others on and off The Hill. Luis Alvarez later admitted that "I frequently violated security regulations by passing along to American citizens information that I believed important to the war effort."[77] Richard Feynman also shared news about the bomb with SEDs in Los Alamos to give their difficult work purpose and a sense of urgency. Feynman had been put in charge of a team of SEDs who had been working on computer programs, but had only produced three programs in nine months. Feynman received "special permission" from Oppenheimer so he could "give a nice lecture about what we were doing." Once briefed, the SEDs were truly excited because they finally "knew what the numbers meant [and] knew what they were doing." In a complete turn-around, the SEDs "began to invent ways of doing [their work] better," were motivated to work overtime, and completed nine problems in three months, equaling nearly ten times the previous rate of productivity.[78]

There was no doubt that everyone who knew the "big picture" at Los Alamos worked harder and faster, but only at the cost of less and less security. Openness undoubtedly quickened the pace of making the bomb, but the lack of compartmentalization made life much easier for would-be spies.[79] In the words of Senator Brien McMahon (D, Connecticut), the post-war chairman of the Joint Committee on Atomic Energy, security in the Manhattan Project had gradually become "a cafeteria service for enemy spies."[80]

Groves' last bastion of compartmentilization also fell when scientists met on a regular basis to exchange information between Manhattan Project labs. The general attempted to limit the number of top scientists involved and the kinds of topic discussed, but to no avail. By August 1943 monthly meetings on plutonium research were underway in Chicago. Additional exchanges and closer contact between Manhattan Project sites occurred by the spring of 1945 when better coordination became critical to the timely completion of the bomb.[81]

Major Breakdown #3: Relaxed Travel Restrictions

Finally, effective security became far more difficult when civilian and military personnel traveled widely in New Mexico and beyond. Despite early regulations limiting travel and forbidding outside personal contact, restless residents increasingly journeyed well beyond Site Y's confines in search of release from the stress of long hours and tedious work. In officially announcing the relaxation of "irksome restrictions" on travel by September 1944, Oppenheimer declared that "There will be no limitations, in time or in geography, imposed by security on travel of project personnel within the limits of [the] continental United States." Permission from supervisors, approved itineraries, and follow-up reports to Site Y's Intelligence Office were still required, but the message was clear: "restrictions which have proved detrimental to morale" were hereafter greatly reduced.[82]

Examples of this extensive travel abound. The military police organized basketball and baseball teams that played opposing teams from all over the state, including Bruns Hospital in Santa Fe, Camp Luna in Las Vegas, the Hobbs Army Air Base, and even the state penitentiary during the winter and summer seasons of 1944.[83] The MPs' teams were said to have "materialized out of a vacuum, trained in a vacuum and after their games [had ended] . . . returned to the vacuum."[84] More casually, two sergeants and a WAC private from the PX and commissary traveled all the way to Taos to pick up fresh eggs one Sunday morning. MPs frequented Taos on gambling excursions. WACs went to Taos to ski and stay at a local ski lodge.[85]

Hugh Richards courted his future wife, Mildred, on trips to the Pecos Valley and Eagle Nest Lake. Following their wedding in Santa Fe, the Richards honeymooned at Carlsbad Caverns in February 1944. On another occasion, three WACs were guests at a ranch owned by a former Russian countess and her companion, a Hawaiian swimmer. Richard Feynman hitchhiked to Albuquerque nearly every weekend to visit his ailing wife at the Presbyterian Sanatorium. Military personnel, including a young tech sergeant named David Greenglass, arranged for their wives to move to Albuquerque where they could visit them on a regular basis. So many Site Y residents went to Albuquerque that G-2 agents were assigned to popular Duke City gathering places, such as the Hilton and Alvarado hotels, to monitor actions and words much as they did at hotels and bars in Santa Fe.[86]

Regionally, Eleanor Jette visited family and went on a shopping trip to Denver in early 1945. Eleanor's aunt was well aware of the Jettes' "secret" home because she worked for Mountain Bell in Denver and had learned of Site Y's location from the arrangements needed to get even a limited number of phone lines up and running to this isolated destination.[87] A gas station attendant elsewhere in Colorado was also well aware of "that secret place" when physicist Robert Marshak and his family stopped for fuel en route to Los Alamos. According to Marshak's wife, Ruth, "He needed no encouragement to launch into a detailed and accurate description of our new home."[88] It seemed that the federal government's top secret project was hardly a secret any more.

A good many scientists and their families saved their gasoline rations for trips to nearby Indian ruins and isolated pueblos. Many, including Oppenheimer, grew fascinated with Indian artifacts and ancient rituals. Oppie often bought cheese and salami at a butcher shop in Santa Fe in preparation for picnics among the prehistoric Indian ruins on Tsankawi mesa.[89] The ranger at Frijoles Canyon saw the scientists and their families so often that he "began to call us by name, although we never signed his visitors book."[90] Other Site Y employees visited pueblos for less cultural reasons: one driver en route to Los Alamos with a scientist passenger stopped at as many as half a dozen pueblos to trade "hard-to-get objects (from the black market, no doubt) for jewelry and blankets and such."[91] Although earlier rules strictly prohibited visits by family members, by 1945 security officers allowed scientists to frequently meet relatives under a designated cottonwood tree at the San Ildefonso pueblo.[92]

Travel to Santa Fe in particular became so common that Otto Frisch recalled "a constant traffic of people who went to town to do some shopping or sightseeing or to dine."[93] Laura Fermi remembered that wives from The Hill were especially conspicuous in Santa Fe when

> They poured out of overcrowded cars and scattered around with hurried, purposeful strides. They wagged their capacious shopping bags and filled them hastily to the brim. They had no time to spare. . . . They bought and bought. All goods that reached Santa Fe in those times of scarcity disappeared into the women's bags, from children's shoes to repair parts for washing machines.[94]

It was impossible for Santa Feans not to notice these residents of The Hill, if only because they were so hurried, so affluent, and so resented for buying up scarce consumer goods at the height of the war. Not satisfied with occasional dinners at Edith Warner's tearoom, many couples ventured into Santa Fe for dinner and drinks at La Fonda and other popular clubs like the Mayflower Bar and Emil's. Even teenagers frequented Santa Fe; in one instance a group somehow commandeered an Army truck just to get to town.[95]

Santa Feans became so accustomed to the odd ways of the scientists and their families that they "claimed they could spot them from a great distance."[96] This was especially true, in an ironic twist, at the annual Santa Fe fiesta. Bernice Brode remembered that residents of the capital "wore fiesta costumes, but since we were not supposed to take part or mingle with people unnecessarily, we wore ordinary clothes. As a result, we were more conspicuous than if we had dressed up, which we [later] learned to do."[97]

Male and female soldiers from Los Alamos could be even more conspicuous by their behavior—or misbehavior—in Santa Fe. WACs like Lyda Speck enjoyed occasional leaves for as long as three days. Tech Sergeant Arno Roensch courted WAC Jerry Stone on trips to Santa Fe, where they enjoyed visiting new friends, listening to records at a music store, walking to the quiet Rosario Cemetery, and talking by the Santa Fe River.[98] So many male soldiers came to Santa Fe that the USO (which could not perform in Los Alamos for security reasons) ran a "flophouse" near the center of town "where a soldier could draw a bunk, a towel, and a bar of soap for twenty-five cents."[99] Soldiers who had had too much to drink often found themselves in a special "chicken wire holding pen . . . constructed alongside the Santa Fe police station to hold misbehaving GIs until they could be transported back to Los Alamos to face military justice."[100] All this activity drew more and more attention to Site Y. In the harsh but largely accurate words of one author, "Anyone with two eyes could have found Los Alamos just by following the trail of beer cans from Santa Fe."[101]

Unfortunately, GIs became even more visible when they courted attractive local girls and became the targets of jealous local males. Soldiers were sometimes beaten up and, in a terrible case of apparent mistaken identity, a sergeant was stabbed to death in front of the Mayflower Bar. Former security guard Burt Sauer recalls that this tragic incident "had the effect of convincing many GIs to carry concealed weapons when visiting Santa Fe."[102] Of course this only increased the odds of another violent mishap and additional visibility for Los Alamos.

When scientists, their dependents, WACs, and other military personnel were ready to return to The Hill from Santa Fe, they could drive their own vehicles, take Army buses, or simply hitchhike home. Many had made the trip to Santa Fe in their own vehicles or had borrowed cars from colleagues. More adventuresome types traveled on Army buses that left from Los Alamos on regular runs from eight o'clock in the morning til 5:15 at night; they could return from the bus stop in front of 109 East Palace Avenue at 6:30 A.M., 11:00 A.M., and 2:00 P.M. Los Alamos buses caused such traffic jams on narrow East Palace Avenue that the local police complained, especially when fire trucks were slowed en route to emergencies. By March 1945 a total of twenty-nine daily bus routes were run to destinations up and down the Rio Grande Valley. Motor pool drivers logged as many as 31,000 miles transporting 294 passengers on 175 trips to and from railheads and airports in February 1945 alone.[103] As Bernice Brode later recalled, "With gas rationing in effect, most of the traffic between Lamy and Santa Fe and Taos was ours."[104]

Hitchhikers were also highly visible in northern New Mexico. When lacking rides back to their mesa, Site Y residents often checked in with Dorothy McKibbin to see who was headed back to Los Alamos. Some simply walked to the north end of town, put their thumbs out, and usually found a ride from a fellow resident of Los Alamos, a construction truck headed to The Hill, or a considerate local driver. W. Franklin Burditt, a SED who arrived in Los Alamos in early 1944, recalled getting a ride from one such local after one of his first trips into Santa Fe. When the driver asked Burditt where he was going, the flustered, security-conscious soldier replied, "'I don't know.' In turn, the driver said, 'O.K., [I]'ll take you there' and [he] did. The civilians were very good about giving us rides" and, apparently, "knowing exactly where 'nowhere' was."[105]

When not busy traveling into Santa Fe in their few hours off from the lab, residents of Site Y explored the beautiful, vast countryside that surrounded Los Alamos. "Exercise," wrote Joan Bacher, "was one way to relieve the high tensions and stress of the Project."[106] Many agreed, participating in a long list of outdoor activities. Some hiked well-worn paths or climbed steep mountains. Egon Bretscher of the British Mission explored the Jemez Mountains with the same enthusiasm he had exhibited in exploring the mountains of his native Switzerland.[107] Herbert L. Anderson recalls a long hike with Enrico

Fermi on the first Sunday after the younger scientist's arrival in Los Alamos. "That hike turned out to be a four hour lecture," according to Anderson. "I was treated to a comprehensive review of what Los Alamos was all about, who was doing what, how far they had come, and what the problems were" that remained.[108] When Emilio Segre and his scientific colleagues wanted to speak freely, they took similar hikes in the mountains and, "as a double insurance of privacy" spoke in their native tongues.[109]

Other scientists, like Richard Feynman and Klaus Fuchs, a German physicist who arrived with the British Mission, enjoyed exploring remote caves "on hands and knees until dark."[110] Laura Fermi also remembers Fuchs on one of the scientists' many picnics held in the wilderness; she found him to be an "attractive young man" with "refined and cultured manners," but otherwise restrained and untalkative.[111] Camps Hamilton and May, purchased as part of the old Los Alamos Ranch School property, were available for those interested in camping trips.[112] Another group preferred fly fishing, and some enjoyed hunting; one British scientist's "desire to take a bear skin back to Oxford [became] the consuming ambition in his life," although few bears still roamed the slopes of the Jemez Mountains.[113] A good many, including Robert and Kitty Oppenheimer, rode either their own horses or borrowed mounts from the herd of about one hundred Army horses used for patrol duties until the last thirty-seven were auctioned off in Santa Fe in February 1945.[114] Winter athletes enjoyed skating on a canyon pond (with music provided by portable victrolas) or skiing on a ski run cleared with plastic explosives by George Kistiaskowsky, a ski enthusiast and, coincidentally, a leading expert on explosives in the making of the bomb. A crude rope tow pulled skiers to the top of the mountain between ski runs.[115]

Most of these travels in the region, to Santa Fe, and in the surrounding countryside seemed harmless enough and much-deserved after weeks and months of labor in Los Alamos. But the greater the number of scientists and military personnel away from The Hill, the greater the opportunity for curious onlookers to do harm to the scientists or to discover the mission of the erstwhile mysterious Site Y. Maintaining tight surveillance over so many individuals moving in so many directions was impossible. There were simply not enough agents to tail every scientist and listen for every off-handed remark uttered while hiking on back trails or eating in crowded city restaurants. On the other hand, exposed with little protection away from The Hill, scientists and their families were extremely vulnerable to kidnappings and even assassinations attempted on busy city streets, on isolated rural roads, or in wilderness surroundings. Oppenheimer, with his trips outside Los Alamos to Jean Tatlock's apartment in San Francisco, to Edith Warner's tearoom, to Santa Fe butcher shops, to Indian pueblos, and on wilderness riding paths, seemed particularly vulnerable. The charismatic director's famous porkpie hat and omnipresent pipe made him a highly visible potential target.

Such intrigue may sound alarmist and far-fetched in retrospect, but it is now apparent that the same military officers in charge of security at Los Alamos during the war were in the thick of planning the kidnapping and assassination of fascist scientists in Europe. If American agents under General Groves could scheme to murder scientists like Germany's top physicist Werner Heisenberg when he was most vulnerable on a December 1944 trip to neutral Zurich, Switzerland, weren't scientists like Oppenheimer, Feynman, and Fermi just as vulnerable to enemy plots while dining in Santa Fe, hitchhiking to Albuquerque, visiting Indian ruins, and hiking wilderness trails?[116]

Top scientists from Los Alamos were most vulnerable to enemy mischief when they traveled throughout the United States on official Manhattan Project business. Despite early precautions about individuals like Feynman traveling in the same trains to the same destinations, scientists often traveled on the same regularly scheduled trains in the same regularly reserved compartments during the war. Groves himself always traveled on the Super Chief, Compartment #101, when traveling on business out West.[117] It did not take a super sleuth to study passenger lists and draw conclusions about these hardly-mysterious travelers and their frequent destinations.

To make matters worse, traveling scientists were assigned pseudonyms that were easy to deduce by even novice spies. Foolishly, the initials of each code name were almost always identical to the initials of each scientist's real name. Moreover, pseudonyms were often unimaginative, usually sounding much like the scientists' real names down to a similar number of syllables; foreign-sounding names were often simply Anglicized. A.H. Compton thus became A.H. Comstock, and Enrico Fermi became Henry (and sometimes Eugene) Farmer, although Enrico means Henry in Italian and Fermi hardly passed as an Anglo with his heavy Italian accent. Compton had so many code names that he understandably forgot which name he had been assigned on a late night plane trip to Hanford, Washington. When a stewardess asked Compton his name, all he could remember was that he "had been given the name of some dark color. Was it Black or Brown? Fortunately, I guessed right and the stewardess let me pass."[118] The scientists' true identity could hardly have been clearer in some cases or confusing in others. Their safety could not have been more jeopardized had there been a genuine threat.[119]

The code names of vital materials and forms of equipment were also quite obvious. Referring to uranium as "ure" or uranium fission as "urchin fashion" fooled no one. According to one historian, "Most of the scientific codes were transparent to anyone with a college-level background in chemistry and physics and the desire to make sense of the project." In addition, codes were constantly changing. Scientists and technicians "strove to remember the changes, [but only] with mixed success." Codes were fluid, sometimes forgotten, and frequently broken. Confusion reigned.[120]

Lax travel restrictions allowed Soviet spies at Los Alamos to travel quite freely to make contact with their assigned foreign handlers. The Army's Counter-Intelligence Corps simply could not keep up with the number of scientists and the range of their travels in 1944 and 1945. The CIC accumulated considerable evidence on a handful of scientists with suspicious backgrounds and extensive travel records. But the CIC's evidence was sometimes incomplete and often erroneous, targeting the wrong suspects while true spies went about their nefarious business undetected. This was clearly the case with a future Nobel Peace Prize laureate, Joseph Rotblat.

The CIC had good reason to suspect Joseph Rotblat during his service at Los Alamos. As a Polish member of the British Mission, he was one of many foreign scientists who did not undergo the Army's security clearance procedure, as poor as that procedure could be. Moreover, Rotblat had refused to become a British citizen, although British citizenship was a precondition for inclusion in the British Mission to Los Alamos. Only James Chadwick, the esteemed chief of the British Mission, was able to garner permission for Rotblat to join his fellow scientists at work on the Manhattan Project.[121]

Rotblat arrived in the United States in early 1944. By late 1944 he was suspected of espionage, especially when he announced that he was returning to Europe because Allied intelligence had confirmed that Germany was no longer committed to building an atomic bomb. With the fear of a German bomb eliminated, Rotblat "could no longer justify to himself the creation of the atomic bomb by any country—or at least his participation in it."[122] American security officers wondered if Rotblat was eager to return to Poland to "tell . . . all he knew about . . . the Los Alamos project."[123] The scientist's eagerness to leave with the knowledge he had accumulated seemed suspicious enough to most security officers.

And American agents had more evidence against Rotblat. Called to a meeting with James Chadwick and Peer de Silva, Rotblat arrived to find an inch-thick security file containing supposedly damaging material against him. Reading aloud, de Silva reviewed each page of evidence documenting Rotblat's alleged contacts with persons in Santa Fe and other locales. The times, dates, and places of these unauthorized encounters were listed in detail. "They were people I've never heard of," said Rotblat later. "It was pure imagination. Fortunately for me I could show straightaway that at the times I was supposed to be there [in unreported meetings], many people knew where I was."[124] After some discussion, de Silva finally agreed that his information was unreliable. The officer apologized and promised to destroy most of Rotblat's file.

But bits of evidence were accurate and damning. Beginning in mid-1944 Rotblat had regularly met with Elsbeth Grant, a twenty-two-year-old former student of his who had recently moved to Santa Fe. Always opposed to what he called "unnecessary bureaucracy," Rotblat had never bothered to inform de Silva's security office of his visits to Grant. Rotblat appeared even more suspicious when he asked another woman to mail letters for him in Santa Fe, despite regulations that required him to mail all correspondence from mail drops at Site Y. Aileen O'Bryan mailed Rotblat's letters and reportedly heard him discuss far-fetched plans to return to England, join the Royal Air Force, and parachute into his native Poland to deliver the secret of the atomic bomb into Soviet hands.[125]

Rotblat claimed that "ninety-nine percent" of these accusations were false, but admitted that "they had something on me" in terms of his unauthorized visits and his mailing letters outside Los Alamos. Any number of Manhattan Project scientists were guilty of similar transgressions, but de Silva and his fellow security officers sought to use this evidence against Rotblat to rid themselves of a current or potential problem. With few options, Rotblat agreed to leave Los Alamos (as he had already planned), but without contacting his Site Y colleagues or discussing his disaffection over the bomb with them, in keeping with Groves' desire to avoid resentment among those who remained. Rotblat left Los Alamos on December 8, 1944, simply telling friends that he was anxious for his wife's safety in Poland. Tragically, Rotblat's wife had already been murdered by the Nazis.[126]

If intelligence officers really believed that Rotblat was capable of compromising the secret of the atomic bomb, they had just released him and given him the opportunity to do what they feared most. But Rotblat never went that far. In fact, in one of the greatest ironies of Manhattan Project security, Rotblat became the only former Los Alamos scientist to later win the Nobel Prize for Peace (1995), acknowledging his great post-war efforts in behalf of nuclear disarmament.[127]

The Impossible Secret

Despite herculean efforts by security guards, American intelligence, and the FBI, maintaining the absolute secrecy of Los Alamos had proven impossible. The project had simply grown too large and complex to control with the resources at hand and the security system in place. As any burglar knows, the keys to a successful theft, be it of real property or of ideas, are entry, access, and exit. Unfortunately for the United States, Los Alamos suffered several great weaknesses that left it open to relatively easy entry, access, and exit. It was only a matter of time before eager spies exploited these flaws and carried out the greatest theft of the twentieth century, the secret to the atomic bomb.

Security pass identification photo of Brigadier General Leslie R. Groves, commanding officer of the Manhattan Project. Courtesy of the Los Alamos Historical Society.

Security pass identification photo of J. Robert Oppenheimer, scientific director of Site Y, 1943-46. Courtesy of the Los Alamos Historical Society.

Dorothy S. McKibben

Security pass identification photo of Dorothy S. McKibbin, officer manager at 109 East Palace Avenue, Santa Fe. Courtesy of the Los Alamos Historical Society.

109 East Palace Avenue, Santa Fe, where all newcomers first reported en route to Los Alamos. Courtesy of the Los Alamos Historical Society.

Members of Military Police Detachment, 4817th Service Unit. Courtesy of Lawrence Antos.

Guard post at Gate #1, the main east entry into Los Alamos.
Courtesy of the Los Alamos Historical Society.

MP checking a civilian's pass at Gate #1. Courtesy of the Los Alamos Historical Society.

Guards patrolling on horseback. Courtesy of the Los Alamos Historical Society.

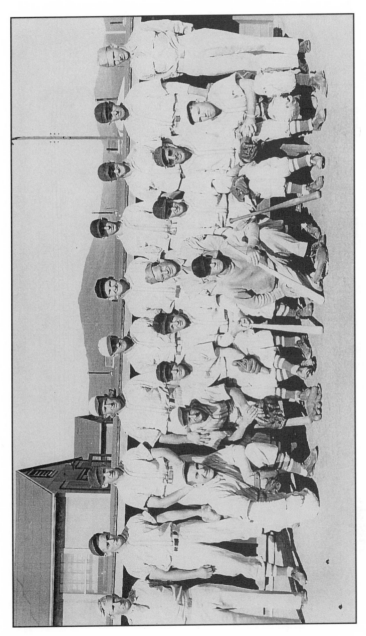

Guards' baseball team. The players' uniforms went nameless, undoubtedly for security reasons. Courtesy of Lawrence Antos.

Post-war photo of Gate #4, the main entry into the Technical Area. Courtesy of the Los Alamos Historical Society.

*Theater #2, site of weekly colloquium sessions starting in May 1943.
Courtesy of the Los Alamos Historical Society.*

*A colloquium session held in Theater #2. First row, left to right: Norris
Bradbury, John Manley, Enrico Fermi, John Kellog. Second row, left
to right: J. Robert Oppenheimer, Richard Feynman, Phillip Porter.
Courtesy of the Los Alamos Historical Society.*

Richard P. Feynman

Pass identification photo of Richard P. Feynman, a vigilant physicist who gleefully discovered faults in Site Y's security system, especially its censorship of the mail. Courtesy of the Los Alamos Historical Society.

Sample envelopes of mail addressed to Post Office Box 1663, Santa Fe, during World War II. Note Army censor's markings.
Courtesy of the Los Alamos Historical Society.

Old Santa Fe Post Office (as it looks today) where all mail sent to Los Alamos was delivered in four designated mailboxes, but especially the famous Box 1663. Army censors inspected incoming and outgoing mail in an office on the second floor of the post office. Author's collection.

Street scene at the southeastern corner of the Santa Fe plaza where many Site Y personnel spent their leisure hours. La Fonda Harvey House Hotel is on the right. Courtesy of the Los Alamos Historical Society.

Check-in desk at La Fonda Harvey House Hotel in Santa Fe where G-2 men were employed as under-cover agents to watch the comings and goings of scientists and strangers to town. Author's collection.

Pass identification photo of Klaus Fuchs, Soviet spy. Courtesy of the Los Alamos Historical Society.

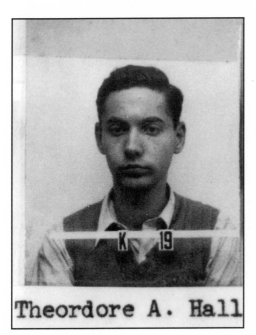

Pass identification photo of Theodore A. Hall, alleged Soviet spy. Courtesy of the Los Alamos Historical Society.

209 North High Street, Albuquerque, where Tech Sergeant David Greenglass passed information about the atomic bomb to Soviet agent Harry Gold in June 1945. Author's collection.

Apartment #4, 209 North High Street, Albuquerque, where Ruth Greenglass lived and David Greenglass visited on weekends, including the weekend of June 2-3, 1945. Author's collection.

Post-war transfer of guard duty from U.S. Army Military Police to civilian personnel. Courtesy of the Los Alamos Historical Society.

3
PROOF

"A stands for atom; it is so small
No one has ever seen it at all.

B stands for bomb; the bombs are much bigger,
So, brother, do not be too fast on the trigger.
. . .
[And] S stands for secret; you can keep it forever
Provided there's no one abroad who is clever."
Edward Teller's poem for his young son, Paul[1]

The U.S. War Department's case against Joseph Rotblat showed both "the reach of Manhattan Project security as well as its ineffectiveness."[2] Preoccupied with what proved to be flimsy evidence against a few suspects like Rotblat in Los Alamos, security paid less attention to the three most insidious threats at Site Y. Klaus Fuchs, Theodore Hall, and David Greenglass were thus free to make contact with Soviet agents through correspondence and meetings that were clearly more dangerous than Rotblat's rather innocent visits to Santa Fe. The cases against Fuchs, Hall, and Greenglass were far stronger than the case against Rotblat, based on their exploitation of the three major defects in Los Alamos' security: poor security clearance procedures, lack of compartmentalization, and the steadily increasing mobility of Site Y personnel.

General Groves' Blinders

But General Groves did not appreciate the gravity of these flaws, much less recognize the three spies who exploited them so well. There were simply too many personnel to police and too few men to handle the workload as time progressed. Government agents looked in the wrong direction at critical moments because they lacked the resources to look in more than a limited number of directions at one time. Groves compounded these troubles by suffering from what his own chief of security described as a fixation on certain suspects; preoccupied with some, Groves wore blinders to other, more serious threats. This was true in the case of Joseph Rotblat and a handful of others, but it was truest in the case of Leo Szilard at the Manhattan Project's Met Lab in Chicago.[3]

Among atomic scientists, only Oppenheimer received more scrutiny during World War II. Like so many of his Manhattan Project colleagues, Szilard was a world-renowned theoretical physicist. Fleeing Hungary (where he was born and raised) and Nazi Germany (where he had completed his university studies), Szilard first migrated to England in 1933 and then to the United States by the late 1930s. Szilard was, in fact, largely responsible for urging Albert Einstein to write his famous letter of August 2, 1939, warning President Franklin Roosevelt of German interest in building the world's first atomic bomb.[4]

Despite their common goal to complete an atomic bomb before the Germans, Szilard and Groves fought each other from the moment they met in 1942. Szilard represented everything that Groves disliked about scientists, beginning with his insistence on the freedom of academic speech. Meanwhile, Groves represented everything that Szilard hated about the military with all its rules and regulations.[5] Suspicious of Szilard's every move and convinced that he was at most an enemy spy and at least a bad influence on others, Groves was heard to say that "the entire project would have been better off if Leo Szilard had simply disappeared."[6] Another scientist recalled

Groves saying that "so far as I was concerned [Szilard] might just as well have walked the plank!"[7] In truth, Szilard was a contentious, brash individual who defied authority and took pleasure in his favorite pastime of "baiting brass hats."[8] And Groves was easily baited.

As the war progressed, the general and his security team attempted to transfer Szilard, force his resignation, intern him as an "enemy alien," or place him under close surveillance for months at a time. His letters, phone calls, and daily behavior were closely monitored. Army counterintelligence reports revealed minute details about Szilard's habits, including that he had

> a fondness for delicacies and frequently makes purchases in delicatessen stores, usually eats his breakfast in drug stores and other meals in restaurants, walks a great deal when he cannot secure a taxi, usually is shaved in a barber shop, speaks occasionally in a foreign tongue, and associates mostly with people of Jewish extraction.[9]

With such meager evidence, Manhattan Project security officers suggested that their surveillance of Szilard be terminated. But Groves persisted, saying that "One letter or phone call in three months would be sufficient for the passing of vital information."[10] To Groves, "anyone who caused him as much pain as Leo Szilard must be a spy. It followed that he ought to be watched."[11] Unfortunately, it also followed that valuable resources were committed to the general's personal vendetta against a single scientist. As with Joseph Rotblat, American agents focused on the wrong suspect based less on firm evidence and more on Groves' biases. Foreign agents could not have planted better decoys to distract Groves and his staff while Fuchs, Hall, and Greenglass went about their work unnoticed and unopposed.

Soviet Spy #1: Klaus Fuchs

Klaus Fuchs' case supports this assertion well. Born and raised in Germany, Emil Julius Klaus Fuchs had become an active member of the Communist Party as a student at the University of Kiel and, after 1933, as a young scientist and refugee in England. Although acknowledged as a Communist alien and detained on the Isle of Man in Canada in 1940, Fuchs was one of several exiled German physicists allowed to work on England's Tube Alloys Project, the British code name for its early atomic research.[12] Years later, the British concluded that "a KGB mole inside M15 [the British security office] had arranged for Fuch's [sic] Communist leanings to be overlooked" when he received his British security clearance.[13] Exploiting his research role in England, Fuchs readily volunteered to spy for the Soviet Union, passing valuable information to his Communist couriers long before his transfer to the United States. Fuchs' espionage was never detected, as proven when he was dispatched as one of the twenty-two British scientists destined for Los Alamos. Having to accept British clearance as its own, the United States granted Fuchs' top security clearance and in August 1944 sent him to work in the most secret sector of the entire Manhattan Project, Site Y's Tech Area.[14]

Finding him an amicable, helpful colleague, American scientists were willing to share much of what they knew with Fuchs. "I rather liked him," wrote Edward Teller. "It was easy and pleasant to discuss my work with him."[15] Richard Feynman counted the 5'9" bespectacled German as one of his closest friends on The Hill. Mothers, including Mici Teller, trusted him so much that they sometimes asked this good-natured bachelor to baby-sit for their children.[16] Quiet, as Laura Fermi had observed, Fuchs was described as "all ears and no mouth;" it should be no surprise that his favorite parlor game was charades.[17] Fuchs thus made the perfect spy. Fellow scientist Joseph O. Hirschfelder later described the German as a "very clever guy [who] . . . . very systematically went to each of the laboratories [at Site Y and] got himself placed in a key position" as the editor of a twenty-five volume secret "Los Alamos Encyclopedia" that summarized all of the research done at Site Y during the war.[18] Of course

Fuchs already knew much of this information as a regular member of the weekly colloquium.[19] Wearing what one historian has called a "cloak of invisibility," Fuchs gathered more and more top secret information to pass on to the Soviets.[20]

Klaus Fuchs also exploited Site Y's last major security flaw: its tolerance of travel away from Los Alamos by 1944 and 1945. Fuchs had contacted Soviet agents by way of his sister in Cambridge, Massachusetts, as early as his first trip to Los Alamos. Visiting that same sister in February 1945, Fuchs met with his Soviet courier, Harry Gold, and told Gold everything he knew about Zapovednik, the Soviet code name for Los Alamos. Incredibly, British Mission scientists were never shadowed when they traveled off The Hill; Fuchs thus went unobserved in Cambridge. More blatantly, Charles (Fuchs' Soviet code name) was not observed by G-2 men or anyone else who might have known him from Los Alamos when he drove his battered blue Buick to Santa Fe and met Gold on the Castillo Street bridge (now the Paseo de Peralta bridge) just blocks from the old plaza and 109 East Palace Avenue. Their rendezvous took place on the first Saturday of June 1945. A last rendezvous took place "near a large church" in Santa Fe in September 1945.[21] With his easy security clearance, easy access to top secret information, and equally easy travel to Santa Fe and beyond, it is generally believed that by the time he was done Klaus Fuchs had supplied enough critical data to the Soviet Union to put that nation at least two years ahead in its development of an atomic bomb.[22]

Soviet Spy #2: Theodore Hall

The second known Soviet spy at Los Alamos exploited the same weaknesses in Site Y's overtly strict security system. Unlike Fuchs, Theodore Alvin Hall was a U.S. citizen, born and raised in New York City. A brilliant young physicist, Hall had entered Harvard University at sixteen and was recruited to work at Los Alamos two years later; he and Roy Glauber (another Harvard prodigy) were the youngest scientists to serve at Site Y during the war. Merrill Hardwick Trytten of the federal government's Office of Scientific Research and Development recruited Hall on the Harvard campus in October 1943. Hall dutifully completed a security questionnaire, and received full clearance without delay, based on Site Y's "voucher" clearance system.[23] Oppenheimer notified Groves of Hall's clearance in a brief, matter-of-fact letter.[24] A statement in Hall's file asserted that:

> Theodore Hall will loyally and faithfully work for the success of this project, that he will to the best of his ability secure its benefits to the Government of the United States, and that he will so secure them, except upon the expressed authorization of that government, from all other nations, parties, companies, organizations and persons.[25]

With the Manhattan Project's clearance system already overloaded with work, no one had the time or, apparently, saw a need to delve further into this young man's limited but revealing background.

If U.S. government agents had taken a closer look at Ted Hall's interests, they would have discovered a student who had not only excelled in physics, but had also grown increasingly fascinated with Marxist ideology, largely as a result of having three devoted Marxists as his roommates in Cambridge. Although Hall did not yet know what secret research project he had been recruited to join in the fall of 1943, he readily agreed with one of his leftist roommates that "If this turns out to be a weapon that is really awful, . . . you should . . . tell the Russians." Saville Sax's assertion, and Ted Hall's agreement, came on the very day that Hall had been recruited to work at Site Y.[26]

Once at Los Alamos, Hall was quickly issued a white badge (Number K-19) and was sent to work in the lab. With this top security clearance, he had ready access to "The Los Alamos Primer," to all parts of the Tech Area, and, most importantly, to Site Y's weekly colloquium. In the opinion of the authors who have studied his case most closely, "Working in . . . the thick of the most dramatic developments, Hall would have known almost as much as Oppenheimer about the design of Fat Man," the American code name for the plutonium bomb eventually dropped on Nagasaki, Japan.[27] Exploiting the trust that Oppenheimer and others had placed in him, Hall collected information about the bomb and made plans to transfer what he knew to the Soviets. In his young mind, it was essential that the Soviets be able to build an atomic bomb to counteract the enormous power the United States would enjoy if it continued to monopolize nuclear research and became the sole superpower in the post-war world.[28]

Passing top secret information to Soviet contacts proved almost as easy as Hall's ease in obtaining security clearance and gaining access to information about the bomb's design and progress on The Hill. Hall had no trouble getting time off to meet Soviet contacts in New York and, later, in Albuquerque. As a junior scientist, he was neither assigned a bodyguard nor ever trailed in his travels. Preparing for such travel, Hall and his Communist contact used a primitive book code (in this case based on certain pages of Walt Whitman's *Leaves of Grass*) to arrange meeting times and dates. Overworked Army censors probably never opened, no less deciphered, Hall's coded message. Once set, Mlad (Hall's Soviet code) met his first contact in a comedy of espionage errors that would have set off clear warning signals if American agents had been present and vigilant. Hall's contact (his former Harvard roommate, Sax) was an "unlikely spy," according to Sax's own wife, because he was conspicuous in his dress, in his tendency to make hand gestures as he walked, and in his habit of talking to himself incessantly. Hall's meeting with Sax on the main streets of Albuquerque was handled so poorly that experts say it would have made a true spy "cringe."[29]

Hall's clandestine meeting with a professional Soviet courier named Lona Cohen went much smoother in August 1945. Only a three-week delay (probably resulting from overtime work rather than from enforced travel restrictions) caused complications for Mlad's rendezvous with Helen (Cohen's Soviet code name as Hall's courier) on the University of New Mexico campus. After finally meeting Hall and receiving the five to six pages he had prepared on his summarized knowledge of the bomb, Cohen quickly left New Mexico by train, carrying Hall's documents in the bottom of a Kleenex box.[30]

Lona Cohen's only nervous moment in leaving New Mexico came at the Las Vegas, New Mexico, railroad station where plainclothes agents were questioning passengers boarding her eastbound train. Cohen went so far as to ask a plainclothes man to hold her Kleenex box while she searched for her ticket in her handbag. Not wanting to draw attention to the box, Cohen did not ask for it back as she boarded her train. In her words, "I felt in my bones that the gentleman himself must remind me about this box."[31] Hardly knowing the international significance of his gesture, the plainclothes man courteously hailed Cohen from the platform and handed the tissues up to her in the train, just as she had anticipated he might. Her quick thinking later became "a classic in the genre of nostalgic [KGB] espionage war stories."[32] Lona Cohen's brief railroad encounter aside, nothing in Site Y's security system had prevented Hall from passing vital information to Communist agents, allowing the Soviets to know all the main elements of America's secret weapon within days after it was tested with great success in southern New Mexico.[33]

Ted Hall eventually lost his security clearance at Site Y, but only after the war had ended: censors noted that he had been receiving "anti-establishment" publications and had earlier received a letter from his sister that referred to Hall's work as "something that goes up with a big bang."[34] While officials had focused on these small details in his everyday life, Hall had been free to pass the secret of the entire atomic bomb without interference from government authorities. Not even his being drafted into the Army in December 1944 made a difference; his self-confessed "idiosyncracies" drew considerable attention to him as a "disreputable" SED in Los Alamos, but never as a Soviet spy.[35]

Soviet Spy #3: David Greenglass

David Greenglass was the third known Communist to operate covertly at Los Alamos. As with Fuchs and Hall, Greenglass was successful as a spy because he too secured easy clearance, had access to the weekly colloquium, and was seldom restricted in his movement away from Los Alamos.

As a boy growing up in New York's lower East Side, Greenglass had been strongly influenced by the Communist sentiments of his older sister, Ethel, and her young suitor, Julius Rosenberg. Given Greenglass' admiration for Julius and Ethel, it was not surprising that he joined the Young Communist League in 1938 at the age of sixteen. Although never a leader or agitator, Greenglass remained active in Communist circles and devoted to Marxist ideology, as did his wife, Ruth, whom he married in 1942.[36]

Drafted into the Army early in World War II, Greenglass was taken from his battalion just as it was about to be shipped overseas. Greenglass was convinced that his superiors objected to his efforts to discuss politics and "raise the red flag" among his fellow soldiers.[37] Instead, and much to his surprise, Greenglass was sent to work as a machinist at Oak Ridge and, later, at Los Alamos where he passed security clearance without a hitch. As one historian of Army surveillance has bluntly concluded, "If the army was truly concerned about security [in the Manhattan Project], it should have been able to detect the sentiments of this young recruit before it sent him to Los Alamos."[38] A short interview with him or with any of his officers or fellow GIs would have been enough to reveal Greenglass' true political stripe. But nothing stopped Greenglass' security check. Greenglass' skill as a machinist was apparently considered more important than his danger as a potential Communist spy. He arrived for duty at Site Y in August 1944.[39]

Having been assigned to Los Alamos, Greenglass quietly but systematically learned as much as possible about Site Y's mission. Rising to the rank of tech sergeant and foreman of the machine shop where the atomic bomb's explosive lens was fabricated, Greenglass showed more interest in his work and the need for security than the average GI. He was, in fact, described as "punctilious" about security rules, or so it seemed.[40]

Greenglass soon began asking scientists questions about their research as it related to his duties as a technician. He often received candid replies from those who were impressed by his admirable interest and curiosity. Eventually, and most significantly, Sergeant Greenglass sought access to the Tech Area's weekly colloquium sessions. Charles Critchfield, a leading physicist and one of the three-man credentials committee that decided who should attend these sessions, remembered that Greenglass "kept bugging us, saying he was as important to the project as anyone else. He said he needed the full story, so to speak." Not impressed, Critchfield and the Lab Security Committee denied Greenglass' request. Not to be refused, the tech sergeant appealed his case to Robert Oppenheimer himself. To Critchfield's dismay, Oppenheimer approved Greenglass' request, granting him entry to all colloquium sessions at Theater #2.[41] Only Greenglass' lack of scientific education and training prevented him from grasping more about the bomb prior to his rendezvous with Harry Gold, the same Soviet courier who had met with Klaus Fuchs in Santa Fe.

In fact, in an unconventional step that defied established rules of espionage, Gold met with Caliber (Greenglass' Russian code name) in Albuquerque on the same June weekend he met Fuchs in Santa Fe. And, like Fuchs, Greenglass had no trouble traveling to his appointment with Gold. For several months he and his wife, Ruth, had rented an upstairs rear apartment (#4) at 209 North High Street in Albuquerque. Greenglass had traveled to this apartment on such a regular basis on weekends that his request for a furlough for the first weekend of June 1945 hardly seemed out of the ordinary. Overtly following security rules to the letter, Greenglass took no documents with him and relied solely "on what he could carry out of the laboratory in his head." The sergeant was ready to meet his Soviet contact, whose arrival and simple means of identification had been prearranged by his brother-in-law, Julius Rosenberg.[42]

Harry Gold arrived at the Greenglass' door on Sunday morning, June 3, 1945. According to plan, he displayed half a Jello box to match Greenglass' half and thus confirm that he was the courier Greenglass had been expecting. Greenglass asked for time to summarize and sketch all he knew about the explosive lens he had worked on so long and now carried in his memory. About six hours later, Gold returned, picked up Greenglass' notes, and vanished into the summer evening. While not as important and hardly as thorough as the information that Fuchs and Hall shared with the Soviets, Greenglass' sketches and notes were appreciated by the Russians who used them to their advantage in the coming months.[43] Never detected at Los Alamos, Greenglass remained in the Army until February 1946 when he was given an honorable discharge, having already received a good conduct medal for his work at Site Y. Years later security chief John Lansdale lamented this security breakdown, referring to it as the "inexcusable Greenglass case."[44]

The Paradox of Freedom and Security at Los Alamos

In one of the great understatements of World War II, Colonel Lansdale later asserted that it had grown "harder and harder to keep the lid on information at Site Y."[45] Incredibly, the difficulty in keeping "the lid on" was less the result of a grand Soviet conspiracy to infiltrate Los Alamos and learn its inner-most secrets and more the result of disloyal acts by three isolated amateurs left undetected by a flawed security system. If Fuchs, Hall, and Greenglass knew each other at all, it was only as fellow workers and participants in Los Alamos' weekly colloquium. None of them knew that the others were fellow travelers, no less fellow spies. They were accidental spies who, to their surprise as devoted Marxists, were cleared and assigned to Los Alamos not through Soviet cunning and expert intelligence skills, but through pure luck and poor security.

There is enough blame to go around in the loss of the United States' atomic secrets, but, as in most such cases, the blame must start and end at the top. It was, after all, Oppenheimer who cooperated in the "two-bit" clearance of many scientists, insisted on the need for weekly colloquia, and allowed for the easing of travel restrictions to help improve morale. Groves was no less responsible: the general allowed easy security clearances (including Oppenheimer's), gave in to the scientists' demand for weekly colloquium sessions, and made little effort to tighten travel restrictions once they had been relaxed in 1944 and 1945.

But could Oppenheimer and Groves have kept "the lid on" at Los Alamos and still have completed the construction and testing of the atomic bomb by July 1945? Probably not. By strictly enforcing security clearance rules, several brilliant minds, including Fuchs' and Hall's, would have been shut out, ironically at the cost of their significant contributions to the Manhattan Project. Moreover, by enforcing compartmentalization, as Groves had sought to do in 1943, progress on the bomb would have been delayed beyond the summer of 1945. What Leo Szilard said of the Met Lab in Chicago, where compartmentalization was long enforced, might also have been said of Los Alamos if compartmentalization had continued there:

> The scientists are annoyed, feel unhappy and incapable of living up to their responsibility. . . . As a consequence of this, the morale has suffered to the point where it almost amounts to a loss of faith. The scientists shrug their shoulders and go through the motions of performing their duty. They no longer consider the overall success of this work as their responsibility. In the Chicago project the morale of the scientists could almost be plotted in a graph by counting the number of lights burning after dinner in the offices in Eckhart Hall. At present the lights are out. [46]

Finally, enforced travel restrictions would have added to the already stressful, crowded conditions at Los Alamos, making the scientists' progress and ultimate success far less likely. Concession after concession had thus been granted by those in authority until only a fig leaf of security remained to cover the location and mission of the project's most strategic site, Los Alamos.

But Oppenheimer, Groves, and everyone else in authority at Los Alamos did the best they could under increasingly difficult circumstances. The atomic bomb was most likely to have been invented in the free society it was meant to defend.[47] Without authoritarian regulations to ensure absolute secrecy, the secret of the atomic bomb could—and was—surreptitiously passed to Soviet agents. Security at Los Alamos had been largely a myth that those in authority agreed to believe—or at least have others believe they believed. As with many security and intelligence operations of World War II, Site Y's security system was little more than an elaborate ruse. While hundreds of loyal Americans on The Hill knew the secret of the bomb and kept it well, in the final analysis Colonel John Lansdale's tragic post-war conclusion was entirely accurate: Los Alamos and its great wartime secret was, in reality, "not so secure after all."[48]

SITE Y SECURITY CHRONOLOGY

August 2, 1939   Albert Einstein warns President Franklin
                      Roosevelt of the possible development of an
                      atomic bomb by Germany

October 19, 1939   President Roosevelt responds to Einstein's warn-
                      ing by creating his Advisory Committee on Ura-
                      nium

December 7, 1941   Japan launches a surprise attack on Pearl Har-
                      bor, Hawaii

December 8, 1941   United States declares war against Japan

December 11, 1941   Germany and Italy declare war against the United
                      States

August 13, 1942   Manhattan Engineer District established by the
                      Army Corps of Engineers in downtown New York
                      City (hence the code name)

September 23, 1942   Leslie R. Groves promoted to Brigadier General
                      and officially becomes chief of the Manhattan
                      Project

October 8, 1942   Groves and J. Robert Oppenheimer meet for first
                      time, University of California campus

October 19, 1942   Groves authorizes the establishment of a sepa-
                      rate lab (eventually code named Site Y) to in-
                      vent, design, and build an atomic bomb

November 25, 1942   Los Alamos selected as Site Y's location

December 7, 1942	Army sends notice of condemnation to the Los Alamos Ranch School
January 21, 1943	Los Alamos Ranch School closes with last four graduates receiving their diplomas
February 1943	Oppenheimer officially selected as the scientific director at Site Y
March 1943	Oppenheimer and first scientists arrive at Site Y
April 1943	Arrival of first military guards, 4817th Service Unit
May 30, 1943	First weekly colloquium meets at Site Y
June 29, 1943	President Roosevelt writes letter to Oppenheimer urging the tightest security at Site Y
July 30, 1943	Groves orders Oppenheimer's security clearance approved
October 1943	Peer de Silva assigned to Site Y as its chief Intelligence Officer
October 1943	Theodore Hall recruited from Harvard University to work at Site Y
December 12, 1943	Oppenheimer tells Groves of contact with Haakon Chevalier
December 13, 1943	First two members of the twenty-two man British Mission arrive at Site Y
December 1943	Censorship officially declared at Site Y

May 29, 1944	Oppenheimer confirms Hall's top security clearance
August 1944	Klaus Fuchs arrives at Site Y as part of the British Mission
August 1944	GI David Greenglass arrives at Site Y
September 26, 1944	Travel restrictions officially relaxed at Site Y
Late November or early December, 1945	Hall meets Soviet courier Saville Sax and, in an amateurish rendezvous in Albuquerque, passes secrets to the plutonium bomb
December 28, 1944	Hall inducted into the Army, having been drafted, but returns to Site Y as a SED
February 1945	In the first of their three meetings, Fuchs passes secrets to Soviet agent Harry Gold in Cambridge, Massachusetts
April 11, 1945	De Silva leaves Site Y for Tinian Island in the Pacific
April 12, 1945	President Roosevelt dies; Harry Truman sworn into office and briefed on atomic bomb
May 8, 1945	Germany surrenders (V-E Day)
June 2, 1945	In their second meeting, Fuchs delivers atomic bomb secrets to Gold on the Castillo Street bridge in Santa Fe
June 3, 1945	Greenglass delivers information about the atomic bomb to Gold at 209 North High Street, Apartment #4, Albuquerque

July 16, 1945	Plutonium implosion bomb successfully tested at Trinity Site, New Mexico
August 1945	Hall delivers atomic bomb secrets to Soviet agent Lona Cohen at the University of New Mexico, Albuquerque
August 6, 1945	Uranium gun-type bomb (Little Boy) dropped on Hiroshima, Japan, by the crew of the B-29 *Enola Gay*
August 9, 1945	Plutonium implosion bomb (Fat Man) dropped on Nagasaki,Japan, by the crew of the B-29 *Bock's Car*
August 15, 1945	Japan surrenders (V-J Day), ending World War II
September 19, 1945	In their last meeting, Fuchs passes additional secrets to Gold "near a large church" in Santa Fe
October 16, 1945	Oppenheimer resigns as the scientific director of Site Y
December 5, 1945	Censorship ended at Site Y
February 28, 1946	Tech Sergeant David Greenglass receives an honorable discharge from the Army
August 1, 1946	Atomic Energy Commission (AEC) created to oversee the United States' post-war nuclear development program
September 1, 1947	Army guards replaced by civilian personnel

August 29, 1949	Soviet Union explodes its first atomic bomb
March 1, 1950	Fuchs convicted of espionage in England; given maximum 14-year sentence and serves nine
April 5, 1951	Julius and Ethel Rosenberg convicted of espionage in the U.S.; sentenced to be executed in the electric chair
April 1951	Greenglass also convicted of espionage in the U.S., but receives a 15-year sentence and serves to 1960
June 19, 1953	Julius and Ethel Rosenberg executed at Sing Sing Prison, New York
December 23, 1953	AEC suspends Oppenheimer's security clearance
June 29, 1954	By a 4-1 margin, the AEC votes not to restore Oppenheimer's security clearance
February 18, 1957	Los Alamos becomes an open city with no passes required for entry; New Mexico Governor Edwin L. Mechem is the first person admitted without an official pass
April 5, 1963	Oppenheimer declared the winner of the AEC's Enrico Fermi Award, the highest honor the AEC can bestow, exonerating him after his losing his security clearance nine years earlier

SAMPLE FORMAL AND INFORMAL MANHATTAN PROJECT CODE NAMES

Name or Word:	*Code Name*:
Hans Bethe	Howard Battle
Niels Bohr	Nicolas Baker
James Chadwick	James Chaffe
Arthur Holly Compton	A.H. Comas (also A.H. Constock, A. Holly, Mr. Black)
Enrico Fermi	Henry (or Eugene) Farmer
Ernest O. Lawrence	Earl Lawson (later Oscar Wilde)
J. Robert Oppenheimer	James Oberhelm
Edward Teller	Ed Tilden
Harold Urey	Mr. Smith
John von Neumann	Mr. Newman
Eugene Wigner	Mr. Wagner
Atomic bomb project as a whole	Manhattan Project
Hanford, Washington	Site W
Oak Ridge, Tennessee	Site X (or Dogpatch)
Los Alamos, New Mexico	Site Y
bomb testing site	Site Z (or Trinity)
Uranium	T (or tube-alloy or tuballyl compound or ure)
Uranium 233	23
Uranium 235	25 (or T235 or tenure)
Plutonium 239	49
Plutonium 240	410
Shipments by water	Freight
Shipments by air	Air
Tinian Island, Pacific Ocean	Destination

Supplies for assembly of weapon	Kit
Core and tamper of implosion bomb	Pit
Bomb assembly team	Pit team
Implosion bomb	Fat Man
Fat Man model	1560
Gun assembly bomb	Little Boy
Little Boy model	1721
atom	top*
bomb	boat*
atomic bomb	topic boat (or the gadget)*
uranium fission	urchin fashion*
atom smashing	spinning*
isotope of uranium	igloo of urchin*
chemist	stinker*
physicist	fizzlers*

*Informal code names

NOTES

Preface

1. Bernard Asbell, *When F.D.R. Died* (New York: New American Library, 1961): 102-7.

2. Harry Truman quoted in Richard Rhodes, *The Making of the Atomic Bomb* (New York: Simon and Schuster, 1986): 617.

3. While still a U.S. senator from Missouri and chair of the powerful Senate Committee to Investigate the National Defense Program (better known as the Truman Committee), the future president had attempted to investigate the unaccounted millions of dollars devoted to the Manhattan Project. Only Secretary of War Stimson's intervention had prevented Truman's further inquiry. David McCullough, *Truman* (New York: Simon and Schuster, 1992): 289-90 and 379. The transcript of Truman and Stimson's telephone conversation of July 17, 1943, regarding this issue is included as Document 10 in Michael B. Stoff, Jonathan F. Fanton, and R. Hal Williams, eds, *The Manhattan Project: A Documentary Introduction to the Atomic Age* (New York: McGraw-Hill, 1991): 39-40. Later, Manhattan Project officials realized that they needed to share their secret with key Congressional leaders in both the House of Representatives and the Senate. Vincent C. Jones, *Manhattan: The Army and the Atomic Bomb* (Washington, D.C.: Center of Military History, 1985): 272–75. The Manhattan Project derived its code name from the location of its original offices in downtown Manhattan in New York City. Its name helped to disguise its later locations across the U.S., especially in far-off Los Alamos.

4. Harry S. Truman, *Memoirs by Harry S. Truman: Year of Decision* (Garden City, New York: Doubleday, 1955): 19.

5. McCullough, *Truman*, 390-97 and 443; Gar Alperovitz, *Atomic Diplomacy: Hiroshima and Potsdam*, rev. ed. (New York: Penguin, 1985).

6. Hanford's critical role was to produce large amounts of Plutonium-239. Oak Ridge's equally important role was to separate Uranium-235 from Uranium-238. "These elements were fissionable, or capable of a chain reaction, and under the right circumstances it was hoped they could be made to produce an explosion that would rival the force of an earthquake or volcano." James W. Kunetka, *City of Fire: Los Alamos and the Birth of the Atomic Age, 1943-1945* (Englewood Cliffs: Prentice-Hall, 1978): 5. It was left to Los Alamos to invent, design, and construct the new super weapon. Rhodes, *Making of the Atomic Bomb*, 486 and 496-97. For wartime security at Hanford, see S.L. Sanger, *Working On the Bomb: An Oral History of World War II Hanford* (Portland: Portland State University, 1995): 138-41 and passim. For wartime security at Oak Ridge, see Charles W. Johnson and Charles O. Johnson, *City Behind a Fence: Oak Ridge, Tennessee, 1942-1946* (Knoxville: University of Tennessee Press, 1981): chapter 5, 137-66. Site Y at Los Alamos went by several names, including Project Y, the Zia Project, and simply Santa Fe.

7. On German wartime efforts to develop an atomic bomb, see David C. Cassidy, *Uncertainty: The Life and Science of Werner Heisenberg* (New York: W.H. Freeman, 1992). On recently revealed Japanese efforts to build a similar weapon, see the *Albuquerque Journal*, June 1, 1997. Neither country's efforts were ever more than preliminary.

8. The five best books on Los Alamos and the Manhattan Project are Rhodes, *Making of the Atomic Bomb*; Kunetka, *City of Fire*; David Hawkins, Edith C. Truslow, and Ralph Carlisle Smith, *Project Y: The Los Alamos Story* (Los Angeles: Tomash Publishers, 1983); Lillian Hoddeson, Paul W. Henriksen, Roger A. Meade, and Catherine Westfall, *Critical Assembly: A Technical History of Los Alamos during the Oppenheimer Years, 1943-1945* (New York: Cambridge University Press, 1993); Peter Bacon Hales, *Atomic Spaces: Living on the Manhattan Project* (Urbana: University of Illinois Press, 1997).

9. Novels include Dexter Masters, *The Accident* (New York: Alfred A. Knopf, 1965); Thomas McMahon, *Principles of American Nuclear Chemistry: A Novel* (Boston: Little, Brown and Company, 1970); Mark

Elder, *The Prometheus Operation* (New York: McGraw-Hill, 1980); Larry Bograd, *Los Alamos Light* (New York: Farrar Straus Giroux, 1983); James Thackara, *America's Children* (London: Chatto and Windus, 1984); Martin Cruz Smith, *Stallion Gate* (New York: Ballantine Books, 1986); Joseph Kanon, *Los Alamos* (New York: Broadway Books, 1997). Hollywood movies include *The Atomic City* (1952) and *Fat Man and Little Boy* (1989).

10. See, for example, Pavel Sudoplatov and Anatoli Sudoplatov, *Special Tasks: The Memoirs of an Unwanted Witness—A Soviet Spymaster* (Boston: Little, Brown and Company, 1994); John Earl Haynes and Harvey Klehr, *Venona* (New Haven: Yale University Press, 1999); Allen Weinstein and Alexander Vassiliev, *Haunted Wood: Soviet Espionage in America—The Stalin Era* (New York: Random House, 1999). These books were reviewed in William J. Broad, "New Books Revive Old Talk of Spies," *New York Times*, May 11, 1999. The Komitet Gosudarstvennoy Bezopasnosti (KGB) means the Committee for State Security in Russian.

11. Quoted in the *Albuquerque Journal*, August 13, 1999.

Chapter 1

1. Lt. Colonel Stanley L. Stewart to All Project Y Employees, Los Alamos, New Mexico, August 18, 1945, Los Alamos National Laboratory Archives, Los Alamos, New Mexico (hereafter cited as LANLA). For security reasons, all official correspondence in and from Site Y was written on stationary with Santa Fe, rather than Los Alamos, on its letterhead. For clarity, Los Alamos will be noted as the place of origin for all such correspondence.

2. The best biographies of J. Robert Oppenheimer are James W. Kunetka, *Oppenheimer: The Years of Risk* (Englewood Cliffs: Prentice-Hall, 1982); Peter Michelmore, *The Swift Years: The Robert Oppenheimer Story* (New York: Dodd, Mead and Company, 1969). Although Oppenheimer never wrote an autobiography, he wrote a brief sketch of his life to 1954. See Michael B. Stoff et al, *Manhattan Project*, Document 7, 29-32. The best biography of Leslie R. Groves is William Lawren, *The General and the Bomb: A Biography of General Leslie R. Groves, Director of the Manhattan Project* (New York: Dodd, Mead and Company, 1988). Groves wrote of his experiences in the Manhat-

tan Project in *Now It Can Be Told: The Story of the Manhattan Project* (New York: Da Capo, 1962).

3. Devona Perry quoted in Darrell R. Schlicht, "Los Alamos, 1943-1945" (Unpublished ms. in author's possession): 16. Improvements on the road to Los Alamos (by the M.M. Sundt and A.O. Peabody construction companies) eventually cost over $65,000 per mile. *Santa Fe New Mexican*, April 30, 1950; Jones, *Manhattan*, 398.

4. Joseph Albright and Marcia Kunstel, *Bombshell: The Secret Story of America's Unknown Atomic Spy Conspiracy* (New York: Random House, 1997): 103. Oppenheimer was familiar with this area, having vacationed there as early as 1921. Kunetka, *Oppenheimer*, 8-9.

5. Laura Fermi, "The Fermis' Path to Los Alamos" in Lawrence Badash, Joseph O. Hirschfelder, and Herbert P. Broida, eds., *Reminiscences of Los Alamos, 1943-1945* (Dordrecht, Holland: D. Reidel Publishing Company, 1980): 93; Stanley A. Blumberg and Louis G. Panos, *Edward Teller: Giant of the Golden Age of Physics* (New York: Charles Scribner's Sons, 1990): 69. Other locations considered included sites near Los Angeles, California, near Reno, Nevada, and, in New Mexico, near Gallup, Las Vegas, La Ventana, and Jemez Springs. Non-security criteria for the selected site included: a mild climate for year-round construction and outside experimentation, access to sources of fuel and water, easily obtainable land, and sufficient buildings to house an initial staff. Los Alamos met all of these requirements, with the exception of adequate water, as would be realized later. Much of the area was already owned by the federal government as part of the national forest. Most of the remaining land was condemned by the War Department and purchased from local homesteaders and the Los Alamos Ranch School. Secretary of War Henry L. Stimson to Alfred J. Connell (of the Los Alamos Ranch School), Washington, D.C., December 1, 1942, Bradbury Science Museum, Historical Collection (hereafter cited as BSM-HC); Jones, *Manhattan*, 83; Edith C. Truslow, *Manhattan District History: Nonscientific Aspects of Los Alamos Project Y, 1942-1946* (Los Alamos: Los Alamos Historical Society, 1991): 2; Marjorie Bell Chambers, "Technically Sweet Los Alamos: The Development of a Federally Sponsored Scientific Community" (Unpublished Ph.D. dissertation, University of New Mexico, 1974): 54-70. The Los Alamos Ranch School's last four graduates received their diplomas on January 21, 1943. The school moved to Taos, but only remained open until the fall of 1945. At war's end, an ad for the school asserted that it was

"proud that the sacrifice of its orignial unique site was an important contribution to the development of the Atomic Bomb." *Santa Fe New Mexican*, August 10, 1945.

6. Kunetka, *Oppenheimer*, 52.

7. Nuel Pharr Davis, *Lawrence and Op*penheimer (New York: Simon nd Shuster, 1968): 192; Robert W. Seidel, *Los Alamos and the Development of the Atomic Bomb* (Los Alamos: Otowi Crossing Press, 1995): 52.

8. Quoted in Chambers, "Technically Sweet," 127.

9. Seidel, *Los Alamos and the Development of the Atomic Bomb*, 40.

10. Quoted in Rhodes, *Making of the Atomic Bomb*, 451.

11. Oppenheimer eventually recruited such outstanding scientists as (in alphabetical order) Luis W. Alvarez, Robert F. Bacher, Hans Bethe, Enrico Fermi, Richard P. Feynman, George Kistiakowsky, Emilio Segre, Edward I. Teller, Stanislaw Ulam, John von Neumann, Victor Weisskopf, and Robert R. Wilson. Many were (or became) Nobel Prize laureates in physics, including Alvarez (1968), Bethe (1967), Fermi (1938), Segre (1959), and Wilson (1978).

12. Truslow, *Manhattan District History*, 105; Hoddeson et al, *Critical Assembly*, 93 & 97; Jones, *Manhatta*n, 348-49; W. Franklin Burditt, "Life in the SED at Los Alamos," Los Alamos Historical Society Archives, Los Alamos, New Mexico (hereafter sited as LAHSA); McAllister "Mac" Hull interview, July 13, 1998. Some SEDs were scientists of military age who had been drafted while already working at Los Alamos. Many SEDs, including McAllister Hull, used their experience in the Manhattan Project to launch highly successful academic careers. Also see Val L. Fitch (a SED who became a professor of physics at Princeton), "The View From the Bottom," *Bulletin of the Atomic Scientists*, vol. 31 (February 1975): 43-6.

13. Truslow, *Manhattan District History*, 105; Hawkins et al, *Project Y*, Graph 2, 484; Jerry Stone Roensch interview, August 12, 1993. WACs were largely confined to "pink collar" jobs, working as librarians, secretaries, clerks, telephone operators, cooks, drivers, and hospital technicians.

14. Quoted in Lawren, *General and the Bomb*, 78.

15. Quoted in Laura Fermi, *Atoms In the Family: My Life With Enrico Fermi* (Albuquerque: University of New Mexico Press, 1988): 226.

16. Quoted in Chambers, "Technically Sweet," 136.

17. Quoted in William *Lanouette, Genius In the Shadows: A Biography of Leo Szilard* (New York: Charles Scribner's Sons, 1992): 308.

18. Lawren, *General and the Bomb*, 142.

19. *Ibid.*, 98; Lansing Lamont, *Day of Trinity* (New York: Atheneum, 1985): 106.

20. Luis W. Alvarez, *Alvarez: Adventures of a Physicist* (New York: Basic Books, 1987): 128; Kenneth D. Nichols, *The Road to Trinity* (New York: William Morrow and Company, 1987): 152.

21. Quoted in Jeremy Bernstein, *Hans Bethe, Prophet of Energy* (New York: Basic Books, 1980): 78-9.

22. Al Christman, *Target Hiroshima: Deak Parsons and the Creation of the Atomic Bomb* (Annapolis: Naval Institute Press, 1998): 106.

23. Charles L. Critchfield, "The Robert Oppenheimer I Knew" in John C. Allred et al, *Behind Tall Fences: Stories and Experiences About Los Alamos at its Beginning* (Los Alamos: Los Alamos Historical Society, 1996): 170.

24. Seidel, *Los Alamos and the Development of the Atomic Bomb*, 52. A precedent had been set in World War I when several scientists were commissioned as officers in the Army, but spent the war conducting war-related research. James B. Conant of Harvard, for example, was commissioned a lieutenant in 1917, but spent most of his time in uniform working on mustard gas research. James G. Hershberg, *James B. Conant: Harvard to Hiroshima and the Making of the Nuclear Age* (New York: Alfred A. Knopf, 1993): 46.

25. See sample Personnel Security Questionnaire, LANLA; Marian Jacot interview, July 12, 1996.

26. Personnel Security Questionnaire, Charles Ivar Hjelmgren, LANLA; Schlicht, "Los Alamos," 22.

27. Hull interview.

28. Edward F. Hammel to the author, Los Alamos, July 16, 1996.

29. Groves, *Now It Can Be Told*, 145.

30. John Lansdale to the author, Harwood, Maryland, July 10, 1996; Lawren, *General and the Bomb*, 164; Philip M. Stern, *The Oppenheimer Case: Security on Trial* (New York: Harper and Row, 1969): 48-51. Bernard Peters was the Berkeley scientist who Oppenheimer described as "quite a Red." *Ibid.*, 70. John Lansdale, Jr., was born in California and was educated at the Virginia Military Institute (class of 1933). He earned a law degree from Harvard in 1936 and practiced law in private practice in Cleveland, Ohio, both before and after World War II. He rose from the rank of second lieutenant to colonel during his years of service in the war. Metta Lansdale interview, August 21, 1999.

31. Arthur Holly Compton, *Atomic Quest: A Personal Narrative* (New York: Oxford University Press, 1956): 120.

32. Richard P. Feynman, "Los Alamos From Below" in Badash et al, *Reminiscences*, 108.

33. L. Fermi, *Atoms In the Family*, 202-3.

34. Iris Bell, *Los Alamos WAACs/WACs: World War II, 1943-1946* (Sarasota, Florida: n.p., 1993): 4 & 9; Dorothy McKibbin, "109 East Palace Avenue," *LASL News*, vol. 5 (June 28, 1963): 6-7; Hull interview.

35. Dorothy McKibbin, "109 East Palace Avenue" in Jane S. Wilson and Charlotte Serber, eds., *Standing By and Making Do: Women of Wartime Los Alamos* (Los Alamos: Los Alamos Historical Society, 1988): 21.

36. Memo to J.R. Oppenheimer Regarding Special Orders Pertaining to the Various Guard Posts, Los Alamos, May 19, 1943, LANLA; Christman, *Parsons*, 117-18. At least one general also had difficulty entering Site Y. See Groves, *Now It Can Be Told*, 161-62.

37. Captain A.L. Cernaghan, Special Orders, Provisional Military Police Detachment, Los Alamos, May 22, 1943, LANLA; Bernice Brode, *Tales of Los Alamos: Life on the Mesa, 1943-1945* (Los Alamos: Los Alamos Historical Society, 1997): 7-8. The minimum age for security passes was later raised to ten. Sherry Robinson, "Children of Los Alamos," *Quantum*, vol. 10 (Winter 1993): 13.

38. Quoted in Rachel Fermi and Esther Samra, *Picturing the Bomb* (New York: Harry N. Abrams, 1995): 106.

39. Emilio Segre, *A Mind Always In Motion: The Autobiography of Emilio Segre* (Berkeley: University of California Press, 1993): 204.

40. Eleanor Jette, *Inside Box 1663* (Los Alamos: Los Alamos Historical Society, 1977): 87. Also see John F. Moynahan, *Atomic Diary* (Newark: Barton, 1946): 55-6.

41. Katrina R. Mason, *Children of Los Alamos: An Oral History of the Town Where the Atomic Age Began* (New York: Twayne Publishers, 1995): 30; Captain William S. Parsons to Lieutenant Colonel Whitney Ashbridge and A.L. Huges, Los Alamos, June 23, 1944, BSM-HC. The Bradburys were living outside of Los Alamos because, with so many new workers, there was an ongoing housing shortage at Site Y. Norris Bradbury succeeded Oppenheimer as director of Los Alamos when Oppenheimer resigned his post after the war.

42. Phyllis K. Fisher, *Los Alamos Experience* (Tokyo: Japan Publications, 1985): 46-7.

43. Statement of Military Service of Peer de Silva, 0-2-270-745, enclosed in James Boyd to the author, National Military Personnel Records, St. Louis, February 23, 1999; Hoddeson et al, *Critical Assembly*, 438n. Site Y's first Intelligence Officer was Second Lieutenant Curtis Clark. De Silva rose from the rank of lieutenant to lieutenant colonel in the course of World War II. He left Los Alamos on April 11, 1945, when he was given a special assignment to lead security for the detachment sent to Tinian Island in the Pacific Ocean to prepare the atomic bombs for their missions over Japan. Jones, *Manhattan*, 527. De Silva was replaced by Major Thomas O. Jones. De Silva later served in the Central Intelligence Agency (CIA) during the Cold War era. Peer de Silva, *Sub Rosa: The CIA and the Uses of Intelligence* (New York: New York Times Books, 1978).

44. Michelmore, *Swift Years*, 90.

45. Quoted in Davis, *Lawrence and Oppenheimer*, 189.

46. Hoddeson et al, *Critical Assembly*, 96 and 438n; David Hawkins interview, September 30, 1999.

47. Ruth Marshak, "Secret City" in Wilson and Serber, *Standing By*, 8. As a reminder that the information they had learned was not to be shared, military personnel were also read the Espionage Act if and when they were transferred from Site Y. Truslow, *Manhattan District History*, 94.

48. Quoted in Mason, *Children*, 36.

49. See, for example, *The Daily Bulletin*, February 18, 1944. A copy of the security manual was included as an appendix in Jette, *Inside Box 1663*, 125-32.

50. Daniel Lang, *Early Tales of the Atomic Age* (Garden City, New York: Doubleday and Company, 1948): 17.

51. L. Fermi, *Atoms In the Family*, 201. Well aware of the sensitive nature of their work, nuclear scientists had voluntarily censored themselves and their publications as early as 1939. Compton, *Atomic Quest*, 115-16.

52. Davis, *Lawrence and Oppenheimer*, 188; Chambers, "Technically Sweet," 122-24. Paragraph 3 of War Department Training Circular No. 15 (February 16, 1943) allowed for censorship of communications to and from personnel under military jurisdiction. Paul Filipkowski, "Postal Censorship at Los Alamos, 1943-1945," *The American Philatelist*, vol. 101 (April 1987): 347. Censorship at Site Y ended on December 5, 1945. N.E. Bradbury to All Concerned, Los Alamos, December 5, 1945, BSM-HC.

53. J.R. Oppenheimer, Note On Addresses, Los Alamos, April 23, 1943, LAHSA; *The Daily Bulletin*, May 6, 1943; Memo from J.R. Oppenheimer to Colonel J.M. Harman, Los Alamos, May 28, 1943, LANLA; Lt. Colonel Whitney Ashbridge, Notice: Storage of Firearms and Photographic Equipment, Los Alamos, November 1943, LANLA; Restricted Security Handbook, 22 and 24, LAHSA; Filipkowski, "Postal Censorship," 348; Bernice Brode, "Tales of Los Alamos" in Badash et al, *Reminiscences*, 140; McKibbin, "109 East Palace," 25; Bell, *WAACs/ WACs*, 51. Not able to refer to them by their actual roles, staff members began calling physicists "fizzlers" and chemists "stinkers." Jane S. Wilson, "Not Quite Eden" in Wilson and Serber, *Standing By*, 46.

54. Bell, *WAACs/WACs*, 4; Burditt, "Life in the SED," 3, LAHSA.

55. Restricted Security Handbook, 11, LAHSA; M. Jacot interview; Hugh T. Richards, *Through Los Alamos, 1945: Memoirs of a Nuclear Physicist* (Madison, Wisconsin: Arlington Place Press, 1993): 63.

56. Restricted Security Handbook, 10, LAHSA.

57. Ibid, 10-11, LAHSA; Filipkowski, "Postal Censorship," 348-49; Robert Jungk, *Brighter than a Thousand Suns: A Personal History of the Atomic Scientists* (New York: Harcourt, Brace and World, 1958): 116.

58. Filipkowski, "Postal Censorship," 349; Bernice Brode, 1976 note and World War II Censor's Notification, LAHSA.

59. Feynman, "Los Alamos From Below," 112-15; James Gleick, *Genius: The Life and Science of Richard Feynman* (New York: Pantheon Books, 1992): 86-7.

60. Richards, *Through Los Alamos*, 82. For a similar experience, see Bell, *WAACs/WACs*, 23-4.

61. Wilson, "Not Quite Eden," 45; Joseph O. Hirschfelder, "The Scientific and Technological Miracle at Los Alamos" in Badash et al, *Reminiscences*, 87.

62. Wilson, "Not Quite Eden," 46.

63. Burditt, "Life in the SED," 3-4, LAHSA; Filipkowski, "Postal Censorship," 346. See Jette, *Inside Box 1663*, 71, for a photo of the Fuller Lodge skit with these small and large boxes. Censorship was also lampooned in a skit performed by British scientists: "an actor dropped a letter into a slot—only to have it fly out back at him." Ferenc Morton Szasz, *British Scientists and the Manhattan Project: The Los Alamos Years* (New York: St. Martin's Press): 43. On wartime theatre in Los Alamos, see Felix Diaz Almaraz, Jr., "The Little Theatre in the Atomic Age: Amateur Dramatics In Los Alamos, New Mexico, 1943-1946," *Journal of the West*, vol. 17 (1978): 72-79.

64. While the scientists' mail went to Box 1663, military technical staff mail went to P.O. Box 180, Military Engineer District and non-technical staff mail went to P.O. Box 1539, and the military police used P.O. Box 527 in Santa Fe. P.O. Box 2610 was reserved for Manhattan Project headquarters in the Washington, D.C., post office. Filipkowski, "Postal Censorship," 345-46.

65. Shirley B. Barnett, "Operation Los Alamos" in Wilson and Serber, *Standing By*, 92. Rudolf Peierls noted that Groves "had requested Oppenheimer to see to it that his people did not produce too many children, but Oppenheimer did not regard this as one of his duties." Rudolf Peierls, *Bird of Passage: Recollections of a Physicist* (Princeton:Princeton University Press, 1985): 197-98.

66. Mason, *Children*, 11.

67. Truslow, *Manhattan District History*, 94; Lawren, *General and the Bomb*, 144; Kunetka, *City of Fire*, 70-1.

68. Eleanor "Jerry" Stone Roensch, *Life Within Limits* (Los Alamos: Los Alamos Historical Society, 1993): 23; Fisher, *Los Alamos Experience*, 40.

69. Alden Stevens, "Cradle of the Bomb," *New Republic*, vol. 116 (March 17, 1947): 15. Also see Jette, *Inside Box 1663*, 25. The difficult wartime installation of phones to remote Los Alamos was described in n.a., "Communications for New Mexico's Secret City," *The Monitor*, vol. 36 (January-February 1946): 2-9.

70. *Los Alamos Monitor*, June 5, 1983.

71. *Albuquerque Journal*, August 14, 1977.

72. *The Daily Bulletin*, January 28, 1944; Truslow, *Manhattan District History*, 95.

73. See Hales, *Atomic Space*, chapter 10, on medicine and the Manhattan Project; Lamont, *Day of Trinity*, 55. There were twenty-four fatal accidents at Site Y from February 1943 to September 1946. The tragic deaths of scientists Harry K. Daglian (on August 21, 1945) and Louis A. Slotin (on May 21, 1946) were the two most famous, both having been caused by accidental exposure to radiation from radioactive material. See Martin Zeilig, "Dr. Louis Slotin and 'The Invisible Killer,'" *The Beaver*, vol. 75 (August-September 1995): 20-6; Barton C. Hacker, *The Dragon's Tail: Radiation Safety in the Manhattan Project, 1942-1946* (Berkeley: University of California Press, 1987): 73. Of the other twenty-two deaths, seven involved construction accidents, six involved car accidents, and four involved alcohol or drug overdoses. Single deaths were caused by a boating accident, a horseback riding accident, a pedestrian accident, an industrial accident, and a gun-cleaning shooting accident (killing MP Frederick Galbraith on November 4, 1943). Accidental Deaths Report, Exhibit 34, n.d., LANLA.

74. Jette, *Inside Box 1663*, 24.

75. Jon Hunner, "Family Secrets: The Growth of Community at Los Alamos," *New Mexico Historical Review*, vol. 72 (January 1997): 40. Also see Kathleen E.B. Manley, "Women of Los Alamos During World War II: Some of their Views," *New Mexico Historical Review*, vol. 65 (April 1990): 260-61.

76. J.R. Oppenheimer, Note on Addresses, Los Alamos, April 23, 1943, LAHSA; Confidential Memo from David Hawkins to All Group Lead-

ers Regarding Technicians, Technical Writings Outside the Technical Area, Confidential Letters, Protection of Information in the Technical Area, Classified Waste, and Security Administration, Los Alamos, n.d., LANLA; Kunetka, *City of Fire*, 98; Jette, *Inside Box 1663*, 127; Filipkowski, "Postal Censorship," 347; Hawkins et al, *Project Y*, 60-3; Truslow, *Manhattan District History*, 101; Peer de Silva to J.R. Oppenheimer, Los Alamos, February 29, 1944, LANLA; Hawkins interview; Louis Jacot interview, July 12, 1996.

77. Jones, *Manhattan*, 262-63; Babs Wieneke interview, *Remembering Los Alamos* (Video by the Los Alamos Historical Society, 1993); Jungk, *Brighter than a Thousand Suns*, 116.

78. Szasz, *British Scientists*, 34-5; Mason, *Children*, 34; Hoddeson et al, *Critical Assembly*, 109.

79. Albright and Kunstel, *Bombshell*, 105; John H. Dudley, "Ranch School to Secret City" in Badash et al, *Reminiscences*, 10; Mason, *Children*, 7.

80. Richards, *Through Los Alamos*, 56; Fisher, *Los Alamos Experience*, 40; Bell, *WAACs/WACs*, 44; Hawkins et al, *Project Y*, 45.

81. Bell, *WAACs/WACs*, 45.

82. Groves, *Now It Can Be Told*, 57; Hawkins et al, *Project Y*, 46.

83. Kunetka, *City of Fire*, 99; Kunetka, *Oppenheimer*, 52; Lamont, *Day of Trinity*, 55; Tad Bartimus and Scott McCartney, *Trinity's Children* (Albuquerque: University of New Mexico Press, 1991): 45-6.

84. Gleick, *Genius*, 162.

85. Quoted in Lang, *Atomic Age*, 20.

86. According to Frisch, "I was driving...into a canyon and taking an S-bend on loose gravel rather too fast. I suddenly saw a tree in front of me, and, unable to move, saw it come nearer and nearer until it hit my bonnet." Otto R. Frisch, *What Little I Remember* (Cambridge: Cambridge University Press, 1979): 171-72.

87. Brode, *Tales of Los Alamos*, 17.

88. Christman, *Parsons*, 270n.

89. L. Fermi, *Atoms In the Family*, 206; Alice Kimball Smith, "Law and Order" in Wilson and Serber, *Standing By*, 83.

90. Jette, *Inside Box 1663*, 97-8; Robert R. Wilson, "A Recruit for Los

Alamos" in Jane Wilson, ed., *All In Our Time: The Reminiscences of Twelve Nuclear Pioneers* (Chicago: The Bulletin of the Atomic Scientists, 1975): 159-60; Brode, "Tales" in Badash et al, *Reminiscences*, 141; Smith, "Law and Order" in Wilson and Serber, *Standing By*, 75; Chambers, "Technically Sweet," 125 and 128-40; Jones, *Manhattan*, 487. Site Y's three commanding officers were Colonel John M. Harman (March 1943 to June 1943), Lieutenant Colonel Whitney Ashbridge (June 1943 to October 1944), and Colonel Gerald R. Tyler (October 1944 to November 1945).

91. John Lansdale to the author, Harwood, Maryland, July 8, 1996; J.R. Oppenheimer, Note on Security, Los Alamos, May 22, 1943, LAHSA. According to Bernice Brode, "We were not allowed to send children to camp or away to school. If they were already in [boarding] school, they could not come home for vacations." Brode, *Tales of Los Alamos*, 16-7.

92. Wilson, "Not Quite Eden," 44-5.

93. n.a., "Baggage Babies and the Atom Bomb," *LASL News* (June 28, 1963): 4.

94. Carl W. Buckland, Jr., to the author, Los Alamos, July 6, 1996; Roger H. Goldie interview, August 3, 1996; Stephanie Groueff, *Manhattan Project: The Untold Story of the Making of the Atomic Bomb* (Boston: Little, Brown and Company, 1967): 202; Bartimus and McCartney, *Trinity's Children*, 94; Szasz, *British Scientists*, 26; Albright and Kunstel, *Bombshell*, 105.

95. Wilson, "Not Quite Eden," 44.

96. *Santa Fe New Mexican*, August 6, 1945; Mary Jean Staw Cook, "Number Ninety-Nine: Santa Fe, 1945" in Michael Miller, ed., *A New Mexico Scrapbook: Twenty-Three New Mexicans Remember Growing Up* (Mobile: Honeysuckle Imprint, 1991): 14; Alice Kimball Smith and Charles Weiner, eds., *Robert Oppenheimer: Letters and Recollections* (Cambridge: Harvard University Press, 1980): 257; M. Jacot interview.

97. Charlotte Serber, "Labor Pains" in Wilson and Serber, *Standing By*, 62.

98. *Ibid.*, 63-4.

99. Hales, *Atomic Spaces*, 254; Jones, *Manhattan*, 278.

100.*Ibid.*; Groves, *Now It Can Be Told*, 146-47 and 325.

101. Hal Rhodes, *The Woman Who Kept the Secret*, Illustrated Daily (KUNM presentation), April 12, 1982.

102. *Santa Fe New Mexican*, August 6, 1945.

103. *Ibid.*

104. Lamont, *Day of Trinity*, 55.

105. *Santa Fe New Mexican*, August 6, 1945.

106. General Leslie R. Groves to the editor, *Santa Fe New Mexican*, August 13, 1945. To help educate New Mexicans about atomic energy, a special article appeared in the *Santa Fe New Mexican*, August 17, 1945, based on a series of twenty-eight questions and answers.

107. Peggy Pond Church, *The House at Otowi Bridge: The Story of Edith Warner and Los Al*amos (Albuquerque: University of New Mexico Press, 1959): 85-90; Edith Warner's Christmas letters, 1943 and 1944, in *ibid.*, 123-28; Brodie, *Tales of Los Alamos*, 122-23; Kunetka, *Oppenheimer*, 64; Smith and Weiner, *Letters and Recollections*, 280-81. Frank Waters' famous novel, *The Woman at Otowi Crossing* (Athens, Ohio: Swallow Press, 1966), is largely based on Edith Warner's life in New Mexico.

108. Lawren, *General and the Bomb*, 177.

109. Compton, *Atomic Quest*, 183-84.

110. Quoted in Lang, *Atomic Age*, 21. Also see Emilio Segre, *Enrico Fermi: Physicist* (Chicago: University of Chicago Press, 1970): 126.

111. Leslie R. Groves to J. Robert Oppenheimer, Washington, D.C., July 29, 1943, BSM-HC; Lawren, *General and the Bomb*, 177. Bodyguards also served as chauffeurs in order to reduce the likelihood of automobile accidents, given the scientists' generally poor driving records. Jones, *Manhattan*, 268.

112. Brode, *Tales of Los Alamos*, 16. Deak Parsons' house (also on Bathtub Row) was the only similarly guarded home at Site Y. Bathtub Row consisted of five houses still standing from the Los Alamos Ranch School era. The five were considered prestigious because, unlike most hastily constructed housing at Site Y, they boosted bathtubs rather shower stalls in their bathrooms.

113. L. Fermi, *Atoms In the Family*, 202; Compton, *Atomic Quest*, 182-83.

114. John Lansdale to the author, Harwood, Maryland, July 8, 1996; Rhodes, *Making of the Atomic Bomb*, 446.

115. Leslie R. Groves to J. Robert Oppenheimer, Washington, D.C., July 29, 1943, BSM-HC, requested that Oppenheimer "refrain from flying in airplanes of any description [because] the time saved is not worth the risk." Also see Confidential Memo from Colonel Kenneth D. Nichols to All Concerned Regarding Safeguarding Military Information (District Circular Letter MI 44-13), Los Alamos, May 6, 1944, LANLA; Lawren, *General and the Bomb*, 145; Christman, *Parsons*, 134. Scientists were allowed to travel by plane more often as the completion of the bomb became more urgent in 1945.

116. *The Daily Bulletin*, May 4, 1943.

117. Jette, *Inside Box 1663*, 15.

118. Captain A.L. Cernaghan, Special Orders: Provisional Military Police Detachment, Los Alamos, May 24, 1943, LANLA.

119. Groves' Memo to the Commanding General, Services of Supplies, n.p., February 22, 1943, appears in Truslow, *Manhattan District History*, 103-4.

120. Lawrence Antos interview, July 21, 1997.

121. Truslow, *Manhattan District History*, 81; Antos interview; *Los Alamos, New Mexico [A History of Site Y's Military Police]* (Los Alamos: Provisional Military Police Battalion, 1947).

122. Truslow, *Manhattan District History*, 80 and 93-4; Antos interview.

123. Quoted in Bell, *WAACs/WACs*, 19-20. Soldiers were also assigned to guard isolated posts where scientific work and experiments were conducted off the mesa. Marvin R. Davis, Recollections, 2-3, LAHSA. Davis recalls that guard duty became so boring that "we went to the edge of the canyon and rolled rocks over the side to see how far they would go." Other guards were reprimanded for test firing their machine guns from guard towers on at least one occasion in 1944. Peer de Silva to Captain Day, Los Alamos, April 24, 1944, LANLA.

124. Hales, *Atomic Spaces*, 129; Hoddeson et al, *Critical Assembly*, 438n; L. Jacot interview.

125. Captain A.L. Cernaghan, Special Orders: Provisional Military Police

Detachment, Los Alamos, May 23, 1943, LANLA; Confidential Memo from David Hawkins to All Group Leaders, Los Alamos Regarding Technicians, Technical Writings Outside the Technical Area, Confidential Letters, Protection of Information in the Technical Area, Classified Waste, and Security Administration, n.d., LANLA; Lawren, *General and the Bomb*, 176.

126. Bell, *WAACs/WACs*, 22. The same procedure was followed by Dorothy McKibbin at her office at 109 East Palace Avenue in Santa Fe.

127. Lawren, *General and the Bomb*, 132.

128. Brode, *Tales of Los Alamos*, 34. A similar episode was described in Bell, *WAACs/WACs*, 37.

129. Confidential Memo from Colonel K.D. Nichols to All Concerned Regarding Safeguarding Military Information, Los Alamos, May 6, 1944, LANLA.

130. Confidential Memo from Peer de Silva Regarding Safeguarding Military Information, Los Alamos, June 21, 1944, LANLA.

131. Christman, *Parsons*, 119.

132. Quoted in Bell, *WAACs/WACs*, 35.

133. Quoted in Lanouette, *Genius in the Shadows*, 358.

134. Groves, *Now It Can Be Told*, 140.

135. *Ibid.*

136. Thomas Powers, *Heisenberg's War: The Secret History of the German Bomb* (New York: Alfred A. Knopf, 1993): 218. Also see Jones, *Manhattan*, 268-72.

137. Condon's letter of resignation (addressed to Oppenheimer) appears in Appendix VII of Groves, *Now It Can Be Told*, 429-32. Also see Jones, *Manhattan*, 271-72.

138. John Lansdale to the author, Harwood, Maryland, July 8, 1996. Also see Kunetka, *Oppenheimer*, 45; Smith and Weiner, *Letters and Recollections*, 264.

139. Kunetka, *Oppenheimer*, 45.

140. Jones, *Manhattan*, 494.

141.Peierls, *Bird of Passage*, 198-99; Davis, *Lawrence and Oppenheimer*, 175.

142.Kunetka, *Oppenheimer*, 45; Jones, *Manhattan*, 493-94. Groves's copy of Roosevelt's letter appears in Stoff et al, *Manhattan Project*, Document 11, 41.

143.Hawkins et al, *Project Y*, 33; Hoddeson et al, *Critical Assembly*, 209; Groves, *Now It Can Be Told*, 167.

144.Szasz, *British Scientists*, 13. Also see Carol S. Gruber, "Manhattan Project Maverick: The Case of Leo Szilard," *Prologue*, vol. 15 (Summer 1983): 73-87.

Chapter 2

1. Testimony before an Atomic Energy Commission hearing investigating J. Robert Oppenheimer's security clearance, April 16, 1954, Sundt Collection, Box 36, LAHSA.

2. Quoted in Bell, *WAACs/WACs*, 20-1.

3. Albright and Kunstel, *Bombshell*, 106; Stanley Goldberg, "General Groves and the Atomic West" in Bruce Hevly and John M. Findlay, eds., *The Atomic West* (Seattle: University of Washington Press, 1998): 41.

4. Albright and Kunstel, *Bombshell*, 106.

5. John Lansdale's testimony before an Atomic Energy Commission hearing investigating J. Robert Oppenheimer's security clearance, April 16, 1954, Sundt Collection, Box 36, LAHSA; Confidential Memo from Major T.O. Jones to Martin Deutsch Regarding Censorship, Los Alamos, December 7, 1945, LANLA.

6. L. Jacot interview; Filipkowski, "Postal Censorship," 350.

7. Groueff, *Untold Story*, 202.

8. Hales, *Atomic Spaces*, 254.

9. Jones, *Manhattan*, 279.

10. Jette, *Inside Box* 1663, 10.

11. Groves, *Now It Can Be Told*, 147; Hales, *Atomic Spaces*, 255.

12. *Ibid.*

13. *Ibid.*

14. Captain A.L. Cernaghan, Special Orders, Provisional Military Police Detachment, Los Alamos, May 22, 1943, LANLA; Seidel, *Los Alamos and the Development of the Atomic Bomb*, 42; Wilson and Serber, *Standing By*, 59-60. Originally, those entering or leaving Site Y had to sign in and out at the exterior gates. J.R. Oppenheimer to Brigadier General Groves, Los Alamos, June 7, 1943, LANLA.

15. Edward F. Hammel to the author, Los Alamos, July 16, 1996.

16. Claudio G. Segre, *Atoms, Bombs and Eskimos Kisses: A Memoir of Father and Son* (New York: Viking, 1995): 46-7.

17. Hirschfelder, "Scientific-Technological Miracle," 85.

18. Mason, *Children*, 69, 71, 112, and 165; L. Fermi, "Fermis' Path," 95; Antos interview; Albright and Kunstel, *Bombshell*, 105.

19. J.R. Oppenheimer to Brigadier General Groves, Los Alamos, June 7, 1943, LANLA.

20. Quoted in Hales, *Atomic Spaces*, 127.

21. Mason, *Children*, 7, 19, 28, and 60-1; Hales, *Atomic Spaces*, 129; Jette, *Inside Box 1663*, 67; L. Fermi, *Atoms In the Family*, 207; Frisch, *What Little I Remember*, 154.

22. Gleick, *Genius*, 187. At least two children, Jane Flanders and Nella Fermi, played this same trick on the guards at Gate #1. Mason, *Children*, 78.

23. Gleick, *Genius*, 187; Feynman, "Los Alamos From Below" in Badash et al, *Reminiscences*, 115; Hales, *Atomic Spaces*, 399n.

24. Jette, *Inside Box 1663*, 72.

25. Antos interview.

26. Truslow, *Manhattan District History*, 94.

27. Groves, *Now It Can Be Told*, 106.

28. Hoddeson et al, *Critical Assembly*, 96 and 438n; Confidential Memo

from David Hawkins to All Group Leaders Regarding Technicians, Technical Writings Outside the Technical Area, Confidential Letters, Protection of Information in the Technical Area, Classified Waste, and Security Administration, Los Alamos, n.d., LANLA.

29. Antos interview; Davis, *Lawrence and Oppenheimer*, 181. Locksmith Gilbert Garcia confirms that sawing through the shackles of padlocks was entirely possible in the World War II era when the metal alloys used to make locks were not as hard as they generally are today. Gilbert Garcia interview, August 4, 1999.

30. Richard P. Feynman, *"Surely You're Joking, Mr. Feynman:"* Adventures of a Curious Character (New York: W.W. Norton, 1985): 142-44.

31. *Ibid.*, 147; Gleick, *Genius*, 189-90; Hawkins interview.

32. Jungk, *Brighter than a Thousand Suns*, 132; Bernstein, *Hans Bethe*, 80; Hoddeson et al, *Critical Assembly*, 432n.

33. Jones, *Manhattan*, 353.

34. Hawkins et al, *Project Y*, 484; J.H. Manley, "Organizing a Wartime Laboratory" in Wilson, *All In Our Time*, 135.

35. Quoted in Carl Abbott, "Building the Atomic Cities" in Hevly and Findlay, *Atomic West*, 94.

36. Quoted in Stevens, "Cradle of the Bomb," 16.

37. John Lansdale's testimony before an Atomic Energy Commission hearing investigating J. Robert Oppenheimer's security clearance, April 16, 1954, Sundt Collection, Box 36, LAHSA.

38. Hoddeson et al, *Critical Assembly*, 93.

39. Nichols, *Road to Trinity*, 106.

40. Oppenheimer's testimony before an Atomic Energy Commission hearing investigating J. Robert Oppenheimer's security clearance, April 16, 1954, Sundt Collection, Box 36, LAHSA. Hawkins explains that his supposedly radical politics involved little more than "trying to push [FDR's] New Deal programs further to the left." Hawkins interview.

41. Sudoplatuv and Sudoplatuv, *Special Tasks*, 219. A mole is "a high-level agent who is hidden within an enemy's government or military organi-

zation in the expectation that he or she will provide extremely valuable information." Norman Polmar and Thomas B. Allen, *Spy Book: The Encyclopedia of Espionage* (New York: Random House, 1998): 374.

42. Hoddeson et al, *Critical Assembly*, 93-4; Hawkins et al, *Project Y*, 37; Lawren, *General and the Bomb*, 131-32; E. Segre, *A Mind Always In Motion*, 183. Oppenheimer's initial list of forty-four Oppenheimer-approved scientists was included in J.R. Oppenheimer to Brigadier General L.R. Groves, n.p., November 9, 1942, LANLA. The list included John H. Manley and Robert Serber of the University of Illinois, Edward Teller of George Washington University, Emil J. Konopinski of Indiana University, Hans A. Bethe and Robert F. Bacher of Cornell, Richard Feynman and Robert R. Wilson of Princeton, Enrico Fermi of Columbia, and Emilio G. Segre and Luis W. Alvarez of the University of California.

43. J.R. Oppenheimer to Brigadier General L.R. Groves, n.p., November 9, 1942, LANLA. Also see J.R. Oppenheimer to Brigadier General L.R. Groves, n.p., August 7, 1943, LANLA.

44. Groves, *Now It Can Be Told*, 141 and 169.

45. Hershberg, *Conant*, 165.

46. Rhodes, *Making of the Atomic Bomb*, 119-27; J. Robert Oppenheimer, "Autobiographical Sketch, 1954," 29.

47. *Ibid.*; Rhodes, *Making of the Atomic Bomb*, 445-46. Oppenheimer was successful in helping at least a few of his relatives escape from Germany.

48. *Ibid.*, 446; Kunetka, *Oppenheimer*, 17; Michelmore, *Swift Years*, 209.

49. Kunetka, *Oppenheimer*, 39.

50. *Ibid.*, 17; Rhodes, *Making of the Atomic Bomb*, 446-47. Other suspected Communist front organizations that Oppenheimer supported included the Committee to Aid China, the Berkeley Conference for Civic Betterment, and the American Committee for Democratic and Intellectual Freedom.

51. *Ibid.*, 447-49; Lawren, *General and the Bomb*, 97; Michelmore, *Swift Years*, 90; Jones, *Manhattan*, 83.

52. Lawren, *General and the Bomb*, 96.

53. Davis, *Lawrence and Oppenheimer*, 158; Groves, *Now It Can Be Told*, 61-2; Nichols, *Road to Trinity*, 72; Lawren, *General and the Bomb*, 167-68; Jungk, *Brighter than a Thousand Suns*, 142. At least one historian argues that Oppenheimer was selected as the scientific director at Los Alamos by default. According to Vincent C. Jones, neither Ernest O. Lawrence nor Arthur H. Compton, the most logical candidates for the job, "could . . . be spared from his own vital project" in the war. Jones, *Manhattan*, 87.

54. Lawren, *General and the Bomb*, 130.

55. *Ibid.*; Kunetka, *Oppenheimer*, 35.

56. Groueff, *Untold Story*, 49-50; Lawren, *General and the Bomb*, 130.

57. Correspondence quoted in Groves, *Now It Can Be Told*, 63.

58. Nichols, *Road to Trinity*, 154.

59. Quoted in Kunetka, *Oppenheimer*, 36-7.

60. *Ibid.*, 37. For Chevalier's response to these charges, see Haakon Chevalier, *Oppenheimer: The Story of a Friendship* (New York: George Braziller, 1965). The likelihood that Chevalier passed any classified information to the Soviets "seems remote." Jones, *Manhattan*, 264. However, as a result of Oppenheimer's charges, Chevalier was denied clearance for a government job with the Office of War Information in 1944 and was dismissed from the University of California, essentially ending his academic career. Jungk, *Brighter than a Thousand Suns*, 155; Stern, *Oppenheimer Case*, 68-9.

61. Quoted in Kunetka, *Oppenheimer*, 41. Despite this opinion in 1943, de Silva wrote to Oppenheimer in April 1945 that "My service at the project and my association with you . . . are matters which I shall remember with pride." Quoted in Davis, *Lawrence and Oppenheimer*, 190.

62. Quoted in Kunetka, *Oppenheimer*, 41.

63. Michel Rouze, *Robert Oppenheimer: The Man and his Theories*, trans. Patrick Evans (New York: Paul S. Eriksson, 1965): 63; David Hawkins' 1995 interview reported in the *Albuquerque Journal*, September 19, 1999.

64. On Oppenheimer's famous—and tragic—security hearings before the U.S. Atomic Energy Commission (AEC) in 1954, see Stern,

Oppenheimer Case, and Robert Erwin, "Oppenheimer Investigated," *Wilson Quarterly*, vol. 18 (Autumn 1994): 34-45. Former Site Y scientists who testified in Oppenheimer's behalf included Hans Bethe, Norris Bradbury, and Enrico Fermi. Others who defended Oppenheimer's reputation included Deak Parsons and Paul Tibbets, the pilot who flew the B-29 that dropped the atomic bomb on Hiroshima, Japan, on August 6, 1945. See Davis, *Lawrence and Oppenheimer*, 157; Hershberg, *Conant*, 317-18; Christman, *Parsons*, 250; Paul W. Tibbets, *Flight of the Enola Gay* (Beynoldsburg, Ohio: Buckeye Aviation Book Company, 1989): 178. Former Soviet spymaster Pavel Sudoplatov has most recently accused Oppenheimer of being a spy in Sudoplatov and Sudoplatov, *Special Tasks*, 194. Several of Oppenheimer's colleagues from the war era refuted this charge in the *Albuquerque Tribune*, April 18, 1994.

65. Groves, *Now It Can Be Told*, 142.

66. Lawren, *General and the Bomb*, 178. British Mission personnel included many remarkable scientists: Niels Bohr, Egon Bretscher, James Chadwick (the mission's distinguished leader), Anthony P. French, Otto Frisch, Klaus Fuchs, James Huges, Derrick Littler, Carson Mark, William G. Marley, Donald G. Marshall, Philip B. Moon, Rudolf Peierls, William J. Penney, George Placzek, Michael J. Poole, Joseph Rotblat, Herold Sheard, Tony H.R. Skyrme, Geoffrey I. Taylor, Ernest W. Titterton, James L. Tuck.

67. Lawren, *General and the Bomb*, 178. But note praise of the British Mission's overall contribution to the Manhattan Project in Hans Bethe to Carroll L. Wilson (of the AEC), Los Alamos, July 18, 1949, BSM-HC.

68. Groves, *Now It Can Be Told*, 142.

69. Lang, *Atomic Age*, 14.

70. Groves, *Now It Can Be Told*, 377.

71. Powers, *Heisenberg's War*, 239.

72. Jungk, *Brighter than a Thousand Suns*, 120.

73. *Ibid.*, 120-21.

74. Powers, *Heisenberg's War*, 247-48; Jungk, *Brighter than a Thousand Suns*, 121.

75. Powers, *Heisenberg's War*, 241. Three top scientists, led by Hans A. Bethe, argue that Neils Bohr never compromised American security in Hans A. Bethe, Kurt Gottfried, and Roald Z. Sagdeev, "Did Bohr Share Nuclear Secrets?" *Scientific Monthly*, vol. 268 (May 1995): 85-90.

76. Albright and Kunstel, *Bombshell*, 64. The primer was later published in Robert Serber, *The Los Alamos Primer: The First Lectures on How to Build an Atomic Bomb* (Berkeley: University of California Press, 1992).

77. Alvarez, *Alvarez*, 128.

78. Feynman, "Los Alamos From Below," 126-27.

79. Albright and Kunstel, *Bombshell*, 106.

80. Quoted in Lawren, *General and the Bomb*, 268.

81. Hoddeson et al, *Critical Assembly*, 209; Groves, *Now It Can Be Told*, 167-68.

82. Confidential Memo from J.R. Oppenheimer to All Civilian Employees of the Technical Area, Los Alamos, September 26, 1944, LANLA.

83. *The Daily Bulletin*, February 18, 1944, and March 17, 1944, and June 5, 1944; Sauer, "Military Life," 4; Antos interview.

84. *Santa Fe New Mexican*, August 6, 1945.

85. Stone, *Life Within Limits*, 34; Antos interview; Schlicht, "Los Alamos, 1943-1945," 10.

86. Richards, *Through Los Alamos*, 59, 65, and 69; Bell, *WAACs/WACs*, 39; Gleick, *Genius*, 184; Szasz, *British Scientists*, 26.

87. Jette, *Inside Box 1663*, 13.

88. Ruth Marshak, "Secret City" in Wilson and Serber, *Standing By*, 2.

89. Alvarez, *Alvarez*, 129; Cook, "Santa Fe, 1945," 15; Smith and Weiner, *Letters and Recollections*, 280.

90. Brode, *Tales of Los Alamos*, 77-9. Photos of the scientists at the Bandelier National Monument are included in *ibid.*, 78.

91. Wilson, "Recruit," 150.

92. Brode, *Tales of Los Alamos*, 114.

93. Frisch, *What Little I Remember*, 156.

94. L. Fermi, *Atoms In the Family*, 234.

95. Stone, *Life Within Limits*, 37; Sauer, "Military Life," 1; Schlicht, "Los Alamos, 1943-1945," 10-11; Fisher, *Los Alamos Experience*, 170.

96. McKibbin, "109 East Palace," 94.

97. Brode, *Tales of Los Alamos*, 85.

98. Bell, *WAACs/WACs*, 58; Stone, *Life Within Limits*, 37; Stone interview.

99. Sauer, "Military Life," 1.

100. *Ibid.*

101. Lamont, *Day of Trinity*, 163.

102. Sauer, "Military Life," 12.

103. L. Fermi, *Atoms In the Family*, 223; Daily Bus Schedule, Santa Fe to Los Alamos, Effective May 12, 1943, LAHSA; Vehicles Operated by Motor Pool [April 1945], LANLA.

104. Brode, *Tales of Los Alamos*, 17.

105. Burditt, "Life in the SED," 4. Soldiers who were unwilling to give rides back to Los Alamos were sometimes harassed with frequent car searches by MPs stationed at Gate #1. As one MP told an uncooperative machinist, "Well, anyone who won't pick up a GI when he's got plenty of room must be doing something illegal or has something to hide. I'm going to keep tearing your car apart until I find it." Burt Sauer, "Random Recollections of Manhattan Project Days," 1, LAHSA.

106. Jean Bacher, "Fresh Air and Alcohol" in Wilson and Serber, *Standing By*, 103.

107. Szasz, *British Scientists*, 34.

108. Herbert L. Anderson, "Assisting Fermi" in Wilson, *All In Our Time*, 99.

109. C. Segre, *Atoms, Bombs and Eskimos Kisses*, 40.

110. Gleick, *Genius*, 190.

111. L. Fermi, *Atoms In the Family*, 208-9.

112. Truslow, *Manhattan District History*, 95.

113. Wilson, "Not Quite Eden," 52.

114. Smith and Weiner, *Letters and Recollections*, 280; Christman, *Parsons*, 134; Burditt, "Life in the SED," 11; *The Daily Bulletin*, August 1, 1945; Truslow, *Manhattan District*, 81.

115. Bell, *WAACs/WACs*, 57; Hull interview.

116. Powers, *Heisenberg's War*, 249, 381, 386, and 391. An American mission (code named Alsos) was created in the fall of 1944 to learn what progress German scientists had made in nuclear physics. Naming the mission Alsos (meaning "grove" in Greek) angered General Groves who realized how easy it was to connect this foreign mission's name with his role in the larger Manhattan Project. See Samuel A. Goudsmit, *Alsos* (Los Angeles: Tomash, 1983); Boris T. Pash, *Alsos Mission* (New York: Award House, 1969). Pash, who had earlier served in Intelligence under Groves on the West Coast, served as the commanding officer of Alsos. Morris "Moe" Berg was the American assassin sent to murder Heisenberg if the German scientist gave any indication that he was leading an effort to develop an atomic bomb for Hitler. Berg found no indication and Heisenberg was spared. See Nicholas Dawidoff, *The Catcher Was a Spy: The Mysterious Life of Moe Berg* (New York: Pantheon Books, 1994): 197-207. The absurdity of Berg's mission is well argued in *ibid.*, 207.

117. Lawren, *General and the Bomb*, 135.

118. Compton, *Atomic Quest*, 183. On similar confusion caused by Niels Bohr's code name, see Aage Bohr, "The War Years and the Atomic Weapons" in S. Rozental, ed., *Niels Bohr: His Life and Work as Seen by His Friends and Colleagues* (Amsterdam: North-Holland, 1967): 200.

119. There is only one known instance when a scientist's code name was changed because it was recognized as too obvious. At Berkeley, Ernest Lawrence's code name (Ernest Lawson) was changed to Oscar Wilde, supposedly because the playwright Oscar Wilde had written a play entitled "The Importance of Being Earnest." Lang, *Atomic Age*, 23.

120. Hales, *Atomic Spaces*, 247.

121. Albright and Kunstel, *Bombshell*, 100-1.

122. *Ibid.*, 101.

123.*Ibid.*, 100.

124.*Ibid.*, 101.

125.*Ibid.*, 101-2.

126.*Ibid.*, 102; E. Segre, *A Mind Always In Motion*, 189.

127.Albright and Kunstel, *Bombshell*, 86.

Chapter 3

1. Quoted in L. Fermi, *Atoms in the Family*, 222.

2. Albright and Kunstel, *Bombshell*, 100.

3. Lawren, *General and the Bomb*, 260.

4. Rhodes, *Making of the Atomic Bomb*, 13-27 and 306-8; Kunetka, *City of Fire*, 23; Albert Einstein to President Franklin D. Roosevelt, Peconic, New York, August 2, 1939, in Stoff et al, *Manhattan Project*, Document 1, 18-19. FDR responded to Einstein and told him of the creation of the president's new Advisory Committee on Uranium in Franklin D. Roosevelt to Albert Einstein, Washington, D.C., October 19, 1939, BSM-HC.

5. Rhodes, *Making of the Atomic Bomb*, 502.

6. Quoted from Groves' interview in Joseph J. Ermenc, *Atomic Bomb Scientists: Memoirs, 1939-1945* (Westport: Meckler, 1989): 248; Lawren, *General and the Bomb*, 80.

7. Quoted in Jungk, *Brighter than a Thousand Suns*, 120.

8. Rhodes, *Making of the Atomic Bomb*, 502.

9. Quoted in *ibid.*, 506-7.

10. Quoted in *ibid.*, 506.

11. *Ibid.*; Margot Norris, "Dividing the Indivisible: The Fissured Story of the Manhattan Project," *Cultural Critique*, vol. 35 (Winter 1996-97): 17. It appears that Szilard received far more secret information than he dispersed. Years later he wrote that "Hardly a week passed that somebody did not come to my office at Chicago . . . wanting to convey a piece of information to which I was not entitled. . . . All they asked was

that I conceal from the Army the fact that they were the persons who had given it [the information] to me." Quoted in Jungk, *Brighter than a Thousand Suns*, 120.

12. Blumberg and Panos, *Teller*, 107-8; Szasz, *British Scientists*, 87.

13. Ernest Volkman, *Spies: The Secret Agents Who Changed the Course of History* (New York: John Wiley and Sons, 1994): 160-61; Szasz, *British Scientists*, 102-3.

14. *Ibid.*, 87-9; Christman, *Parsons*, 38.

15. Quoted in Blumberg and Panos, *Teller*, 108.

16. Szasz, *British Scientists*, 91; H. Rhodes, *Woman Who Kept a Secret*; Blumberg and Panos, *Teller*, 108.

17. Quoted in Lawren, *General and the Bomb*, 179; Szasz, *British Scientists*, 35.

18. Hirschfelder, "Scientific-Technological Miracle," 85-6. Also see Robert Chadwell Williams, *Klaus Fuchs, Atomic Spy* (Cambridge: Harvard University Press, 1987): 76-7.

19. *Ibid.*, 78-9; Szasz, *British Scientists*, 92.

20. Oliver Pilat, *The Atom Spies* (New York: G.P. Putnam's Sons, 1952): 176.

21. Klaus Fuchs' confession to Michael W. Perrin, January 30, 1950, and Harry Gold's statement to the FBI, May 22, 1950, in Williams, *Fuchs*, 190-91, 199, and 214-15.

22. Albright and Kunstel, *Bombshell*, 107 and 123; Szasz, *British Scientists*, 27 and 88-9. Zapovednik means "reservation" in Russian. The Soviet Union detonated its first atomic bomb on August 29, 1949. Fuchs was arrested, tried for espionage in a trial that lasted less than an hour and a half, and convicted by an English jury on March 1, 1950. He received a maximum fourteen-year sentence, but was released after serving nine years. Once freed, Fuchs emigrated to East Germany where he worked in a nuclear physics institute until his retirement in 1979. He died in 1988. Ronald Radosh and Joyce Milton, *The Rosenberg File: A Search for the Truth* (New York: Holt, Rinehart and Winston, 1983): 12-13; Volkman, *Spies*, 162.

23. Albright and Kunstel, *Bombshell*, 60-2. The average age among scien-

tists at Los Alamos was twenty-nine.

24. J.R. Oppenheimer to Major General L.R. Groves, Los Alamos, May 29, 1944, LANLA.

25. Statement Vouching for the Loyalty of Theodore Hall, March 1, 1944, LANLA.

26. Albright and Kunstel, *Bombshell*, 61.

27. *Ibid.*, 64 and 113.

28. See Hall's letter to Albright and Kunstel, March 24, 1997, included in *ibid.*, 288-89.

29. *Ibid.*, 99, 112, and 114. Mlad means "young" in Old Slavonic. See the "Top Secret, Urgent" KGB letter (dated July 10, 1945) identifying "Mlad" as a main source of information about the American atomic bomb. Sudoplatov and Sudoplatov, *Special Tasks*, 475.

30. Albright and Kunstel, *Bombshell*, 149-52.

31. Quoted in *ibid.*, 152.

32. *Ibid.*, 151-53.

33. *Ibid.*, 121.

34. Quoted in *ibid.*, 166.

35. *Ibid.*, 115 and 128-29. Hall accepted a thousand dollars for his information, but donated half of it to a housing co-op and shared half of it with Sax, "who was in need of funds." Hall married Chicago-native Joan Krakover after World War II and, after living in fear of FBI investigations in the late 1940s and early 1950s, enjoyed "comfortable obscurity" as a successful research physicist in the eastern United States and, from 1962 to 1984, in England. Never officially charged with espionage, Hall returned to New Mexico only once, for an academic conference held at the University of New Mexico in 1986. Hall walked around the campus, but could not identify the place where he and Lona Cohen had met in 1945. He did not go so far as to visit Los Alamos. Suffering from several illnesses, Hall died of cancer November 1, 1999. *Ibid.*, 171-74, 238-39, 256-57, and 266.

36. Radosh and Milton, *Rosenberg File*, 57-60.

37. Quoted in *ibid.*, 60.

38. Joan M. Jensen, *Army Surveillance in America, 1775-1980* (New Haven: Yale University Press, 1991): 237.

39. Ilene Philipson, *Ethel Rosenberg: Beyond the Myths* (New York: Franklin Watts, 1988): 177.

40. Lamont, *Day of Trinity*, 115.

41. Quoted in the *Albuquerque Journal*, May 8, 1994.

42. Sudoplatov and Sudoplatov, *Special Tasks*, 213; Margaret Freeman interview, August 3, 1993. The Freemans owned and operated the apartment house at 209 North High Street in Albuquerque.

43. Walter and Mirian Schneir, *Invitation to An Inquest* (Baltimore: Penguin Books, 1965): 373-77. The Greenglasses reportedly accepted an envelope containing five hundred dollars from Gold. Although also offered money by Gold, Fuchs refused, but later accepted about four hundred dollars after he returned to England. As loyal Communists, neither Greenglass nor Fuchs spied primarily for pecuniary rewards. Albright and Kunstel, *Bombshell*, 174.

44. Testimony before an Atomic Energy Commission hearing investigating J. Robert Oppenheimer's security clearance, April 16, 1954, Sundt Collection, Box 36, LAHSA. Greenglass was a key witness in the government's case against Julius and Ethel Rosenberg. Radosh and Milton, *Rosenberg File*, 181-95; Philipson, *Ethel Rosenberg*, 280. Greenglass pled guilty to the charge of espionage and, in exchange for his testimony against the Rosenbergs, received a sentence of fifteen years in prison, of which he served ten. In sharp contrast, the Rosenbergs pled innocent, were found guilty, and, in one of the most controversial court decisions in American history, were sentenced to be executed. They each died in the electric chair in New York's Sing Sing Prison on June 19, 1953. Radosh and Milton, *Rosenberg File*, 287-90 and 413-19. The Rosenbergs' guilt or innocence has been argued by many authors since 1953. Radosh and Milton contend that the couple was guilty (*ibid.*, 450-51), while the Rosenbergs' sons are foremost among those who contend they were not. See Robert and Michael Meeropol, *We Are Your Sons: The Legacy of Ethel and Julius Rosenberg* (New York: Ballantine Books, 1975).

45. Testimony before an Atomic Energy Commission hearing investigating J. Robert Oppenheimer's security clearance, April 16, 1954, Sundt Collection, Box 36, LAHSA.

46. Quoted in Rhodes, *Making of the Atomic Bomb*, 510.

47. Sissela Bok, *Secrets: On the Ethics of Concealment and Revelation* (New York: Vintage Books, 1983): 197.

48. Testimony before an Atomic Energy Commission hearing investigating J. Robert Oppenheimer's security clearance, April 16, 1954, Sundt Collection, Box 36, LAHSA. For security at the atomic bomb's test site in southern New Mexico (code named the Trinity Site), see Ferenc Morton Szasz, *The Day the Sun Rose Twice: The Story of the Trinity Site Nuclear Explosion, July 16, 1945* (Albuquerque: University of New Mexico Press, 1984): 37 and 85-6.

BIBLIOGRAPHY

Archives, Libraries, and Museums:

Bradbury Science Museum, Historical Collection, Los Alamos, New Mexico

Los Alamos Historical Society Archives, Los Alamos, New Mexico

Los Alamos National Laboratory Archives, Los Alamos, New Mexico

Center for Southwest Research, University of New Mexico, Albuquerque, New Mexico

J. Robert Oppenheimer Research Library, Los Alamos National Laboratory, Los Alamos, New Mexico

New Mexico State Archives and Records Center, Santa Fe, New Mexico

Interviews and Correspondence:

Lawrence Antos interview, July 21, 1997
Carl W. Buckland, Jr., correspondence: July 6, 1996
Margaret Freeman interview, August 3, 1993
Gilbert Garcia, August 4, 1999
Edward F. Hammel correspondence: July 16, 1996
David Hawkins interview, September 30, 1999
McAllister Hull interview, July 13, 1998
Marian Jacot interview, July 12, 1996
Louis Jacot interview, July 12, 1996

John Lansdale, Jr., correspondence: June 18, 1996; July 8, 1996; July 10, 1996; August 30, 1996
Metta Lansdale interview, August 21, 1999
Arno Roensch interview, August 12, 1993
Eleanor (Jerry) Stone Roensch interview, August 12, 1993

Videos:

Remembering Los Alamos. Los Alamos Historical Society, 1993.

Rhodes, Hal. *The Woman Who Kept a Secret.* Illustrated Daily (a KUNM presentation), April 12, 1982.

Newspapers and Bulletins:

Albuquerque Journal
[Los Alamos] *Daily Bulletin*
Los Alamos Monitor
New York Times
Santa Fe New Mexican

Selected Books:

Albright, Joseph, and Marcia Kunstel. *Bombshell: The Secret Story of America's Unknown Atomic Spy Conspiracy.* New York: Times Books, 1997.

Allred, John C. et al. *Behind Tall Fences: Stories and Experiences About Los Alamos at its Beginning.* Los Alamos: Los Alamos Historical Society, 1996.

Alperovitz, Gar. *Atomic Diplomacy: Hiroshima and Potsdam*, revised edition. New York: Penguin, 1985.

Alvarez, Luis W. *Alvarez: Adventures of a Physicist.* New York: Basic Books, 1987.

Badash, Lawrence, Joseph O. Hirschfelder, and Herbert P. Broida, editors. *Reminiscences of Los Alamos, 1943-1945.* Dordrecht, Holland: D. Reidel Publishing Company, 1980.

Bartimus, Tad, and Scott McCartney. *Trinity's Children: Living Along America's Nuclear Highway*. Albuquerque: University of New Mexico Press, 1991.

Bell, Iris. *Los Alamos WAACs/WACs: World War II, 1943-1946*. Sarasota, Florida: Coastal Printing, 1993.

Bernstein, Jeremy. *Hans Bethe, Prophet of Energy*. New York: Basic Books, 1979.

Blumberg, Stanley A., and Louis G. Panos. *Edward Teller: Giant of the Golden Age of Physics*. New York: Charles Scribner's Sons, 1990.

Bok, Sissela. *Secrets: On the Ethics of Concealment and Revelation*. New York: Vintage Books, 1983.

Brode, Bernice. *Tales of Los Alamos: Life on the Mesa, 1943-1945*. Los Alamos: Los Alamos, 1997.

Brown, Anthony Cave, and Charles B. MacDonald, editors. *The Secret History of the Atomic Bomb*. New York: Delta Books, 1977.

Cassidy, David C. *Uncertainty: The Life and Science of Werner Heisenberg*. New York: W.H. Freeman, 1992.

Chevalier, Haakon. *Oppenheimer: The Story of a Friendship*. New York: George Braziller, 1965.

Childs, Herbert. *An American Genius: The Life of Ernest Orlando Lawrence*. New York: E.P. Dutton, 1968.

Christman, Al. *Target Hiroshima: Deak Parsons and the Creation of the Atomic Bomb*. Annapolis: Naval Institute Press, 1998.

Church, Peggy Pond. *The House at Otowi Bridge: The Story of Edith Warner and Los Alamos*. Albuquerque: University of New Mexico Press, 1959.

Compton, Arthur Holly. *Atomic Quest: A Personal Narrative*. New York: Oxford University Press, 1956.

Davis, Nuel Pharr. *Lawrence and Oppenheimer.* New York: Simon and Schuster, 1968.

Dawidoff, Nicholas. *The Catcher Was a Spy: The Mysterious Life of Moe Berg.* New York: Pantheon Books, 1994.

de Silva, Peer. *Sub Rosa: The CIA and the Use of Intelligence.* New York: Times Books, 1978.

Ermenc, Joseph J., editor. *Atomic Scientists: Memoirs, 1939-1945.* Westport: Meckler, 1989.

Fermi, Laura. *Atoms In the Family: My Life With Enrico Fermi.* Albuquerque: University of New Mexico Press, 1988.

Fermi, Rachel, and Esther Samra. *Picturing the Bomb: Photographs from the Secret World of the Manhattan Project.* New York: Harry N. Abrams, 1995.

Feynman, Richard P. *"Surely You're Joking, Mr. Feynman:" Adventures of a Curious Character.* New York: W.W. Norton, 1985.

Fisher, Phyllis K. *Los Alamos Experience.* Tokyo: Japan Publications, 1985.

Frisch, Otto R. *What Little I Remember.* Cambridge: Cambridge University Press, 1979.

Gleick, James. *Genius: The Life and Science of Richard Feynman.* New York: Pantheon Books, 1992.

Groueff, Stephane. *Manhattan Project: The Untold Story of the Making of the Atomic Bomb.* New York: Bantam Books, 1967.

Groves, Leslie R. *Now It Can Be Told: The Story of the Manhattan Project.* New York: Da Capo, 1962.

Gusterson, Hugh. *Nuclear Rites: A Weapons Laboratory at the End of the Cold War.* Berkeley: University of California Press, 1996.

Hacker, Barton C. *The Dragon's Tail: Radiation Safety in the Manhattan Project, 1942-1946.* Berkeley: University of California Press, 1987.

Hales, Peter Bacon. *Atomic Spaces: Living on the Manhattan Project*. Urbana: University of Illinois Press, 1997.

Hawkins, David, Edith C. Truslow, and Ralph Carlisle Smith. *Project Y: The Los Alamos Story*. Los Angeles: Tomash Publishers, 1983.

Hayes, John Earl, and Harvey Klehr. *Venora*. New Haven: Yale University Press, 1999.

Hershberg, James G. *James B. Conant: Harvard to Hiroshima and the Making of the Nuclear Age*. New York: Alfred A. Knopf, 1993.

Hevly, Bruce, and John M. Findlay, editors. *The Atomic West*. Seattle: University of Washington Press, 1998.

Hoddeson, Lillian, Paul W. Henriksen, Roger A. Meade, and Catherine Westfall. *Critical Assembly: A Technical History of Los Alamos during the Oppenheimer Years, 1943-1945*. New York: Cambridge University Press, 1993.

Holloway, Rachel L. *In the Matter of J. Robert Oppenheimer: Politics, Rhetoric, and Self-Defense*. Westport, Connecticut: Praeger, 1993.

Jensen, Joan M. *Army Surveillance in America, 1975-1980*. New Haven: Yale University Press, 1991.

Jette, Eleanor. *Inside Box 1663*. Los Alamos: Los Alamos, 1977.

Jones, Vincent C. *Manhattan: The Army and the Atomic Bomb*. Washington, D.C.: Center of Military History, 1985.

Jungk, Robert. *Brighter than a Thousand Suns: A Personal History of the Atomic Scientists*. New York: Harcourt, Brace and World, 1958.

Kunetka, James W. *City of Fire: Los Alamos and the Birth of the Atomic Age, 1943-1945*. Englewood Cliffs, New Jersey: Prentice-Hall, 1978.

_____. *Oppenheimer: The Years of Risk*. Englewood Cliffs, New Jersey: Prentice-Hall, 1982.

Lamont, Lansing. *Day of Trinity*. New York: Atheneum, 1985.

Lang, Daniel. *Early Tales of the Atomic Age*. Garden City, New York: Doubleday, 1948.

Lanouette, William. *Genius in the Shadows: A Biography of Leo Szilard*. New York: Charles Scribner's Sons, 1992.

Laurence, William L. *Dawn Over Zero: The Story of the Atomic Bomb*. New York: Alfred A. Knopf, 1946.

Lawren, William. *The General and the Bomb: A Biography of General Leslie R. Groves, Director of the Manhattan Project*. New York: Dodd, Mead and Company, 1988.

Libby, Leona Marshall. *The Uranium People*. New York: Charles Scribner's Sons, 1979.

McCullough, David. *Truman*. New York: Simon and Schuster, 1992.

Mason, Katrina R. *Children of Los Alamos: An Oral History of the Town Where the Atomic Age Began*. New York: Twayne Publishers, 1995.

Meeropol, Robert and Michael. *We Are Your Sons: The Legacy of Ethel and Julius Rosenberg*. New York: Ballantine Books, 1975.

Michelmore, Peter. *The Swift Years: The Robert Oppenheimer Story*. New York: Dodd, Mead and Company, 1969.

Moynahan, John F. *Atomic Diary*. Newark: Barton, 1946.

Moynihan, Daniel Patrick. *Secrecy: The American Experience*. New Haven: Yale University Press, 1998.

Nichols, Kenneth D. *The Road to Trinity*. New York: William Morrow, 1987.

Pash, Boris T. *Alsos Mission*. New York: Award House, 1969.

Peierls, Rudolf. *Bird of Passage: Recollections of a Physicist*. Princeton: Princeton University Press, 1985.

Philipson, Ilene. *Ethel Rosenberg*. New York: Franklin Watts, 1988.

Pilat, Oliver. *The Atom Spies*. New York: G.P. Putnam's Sons, 1952.

Powers, Thomas. *Heisenberg's War: The Secret History of the German Bomb*. New York: Alfred A. Knopf, 1993.

Radosh, Ronald, and Joyce Milton. *The Rosenberg File: A Search for the Truth*. New York: Holt, Rinehart and Winston, 1983.

Rhodes, Richard. *The Making of the Atomic Bomb*. New York: Touchstone Book, 1986.

Richards, Hugh T. *Through Los Alamos, 1945: Memoirs of a Nuclear Physicist*. Madison: Arlington Place Press, 1993.

Richardson, Jeffrey T. *A Century of Spies: Intelligence in the Twentieth Century*. New York: Oxford University Press, 1995.

Roensch, Eleanor (Jerry) Stone. *Life Within Limits*. Los Alamos: Los Alamos Historical Society, 1993.

Rosenthal, Debra. *At the Heart of the Bomb: The Dangerous Allure of Weapons Work*. Reading, Massachusetts: Addison-Wesley, 1990.

Rothman, Hal K. *On Rims and Ridges: The Los Alamos Area Since 1880*. Lincoln: University of Nebraska Press, 1992.

Rouze, Michel. *Robert Oppenheimer: The Man and his Theories*, translated by Patrick Evans. New York: Paul S. Eriksson, 1965.

Rozental, S., editor. *Niels Bohr: His Life and Work As Seen By His Friends and Colleagues*. Amsterdam: North-Holland, 1967.

Schneir, Walter and Miran Schneir. *Invitation to An Inquest*. Baltimore: Penguin Books, 1965.

Seidel, Robert W. *Los Alamos and the Development of the Atomic Bomb*. Los Alamos: Otowi Crossing Press, 1995.

Serber, Robert. *The Los Alamos Primer: The First Lectures on How to Build an Atomic Bomb*. Berkeley: University of California Press, 1992.

Shroyer, Jo Ann. *Secret Mesa: Inside Los Alamos National Laboratory*. New York: John Wiley and Sons, 1998.

Smith, Alice Kimball and Charles Weiner, editors. *Robert Oppenheimer: Letters and Recollections*. Cambridge: Harvard University Press, 1980.

Stern, Philip M. *The Oppenheimer Case: Security on Trial*. New York: Harper and Row, 1969.

Stoff, Michael B., Jonathan F. Fanton, and R. Hal Williams, editors. *The Manhattan Project: A Documentary Introduction to the Atomic Age*. New York: McGraw-Hill, 1991.

Stone, Jeremy J. *Every Man Should Try: Adventures of a Public Interest Activist*. New York: Public Affairs, 1999.

Sudoplatov, Pavel, and Anatoli Sudoplatov. *Special Tasks: The Memoirs of an Unwanted Witness—A Soviet Spymaster*. New York: Little, Brown and Company, 1994.

Szasz, Ferenc Morton. *British Scientists and the Manhattan Project: The Los Alamos Years*. New York: St. Martin's Press, 1992.

_____. *The Day the Sun Rose Twice: The Story of the Trinity Site Nuclear Explosion, July 16, 1945*. Albuquerque: University of New Mexico Press, 1984.

Truman, Harry S. *Memoirs by Harry S. Truman: Year of Decision*. Garden City, New York: Doubleday, 1955.

Truslow, Edith C. *Manhattan District History: Nonscientific Aspects of Los Alamos Project Y, 1942-1946*. Los Alamos: Los Alamos Historical Society, 1991.

Volkman, Ernest. *Espionage: The Greatest Spy Operations of the Twentieth Century*. New York: John Wiley, 1995.

_____. *Spies: the Secret Agents Who Changed the Course of History*. New York: John Wiley, 1994.

Weart, Spencer R. and Gertrud Weiss Szilard. *Leo Szilard: His Version of the Facts.* Cambridge: MIT Press, 1978.

Weinstein, Allen, and Alexander Vassiliev. *Haunted Wood: Soviet Espionage in America—The Stalin Era.* New York: Random House, 1999.

Williams, Robert Chadwell. *Klaus Fuchs, Atomic Spy.* Cambridge: Harvard University Press, 1987.

Wilson, Jane S., editor. *All In Our Time: The Reminiscences of Twelve Nuclear Pioneers.* Chicago: Bulletin of Atomic Scientists, 1975.

Wilson, Jane S., and Charlotte Serber, editors. *Standing By and Making Do: Women of Wartime Los Alamos.* Los Alamos: Los Alamos Historical Society, 1988.

Selected Articles:

Bethe, Hans A., and Kurt Gottfried, and Roald Z. Sagdeev. "Did Bohr Share Nuclear Secrets?" *Scientific Monthly*, vol. 268 (May 1995): 85-90.

Erwin, Robert. "Oppenheimer Investigated." *Wilson Quarterly*, vol. 18 (Autumn 1994): 34-45.

Filipkowski, Paul. "Postal Censorship at Los Alamos, 1943-1945." *The American Philatelist*, vol. 101 (April 1987): 345-50.

Fitch, Val L. "The View From the Bottom." *Bulletin of the Atomic Scientists*, vol. 31 (February 1975): 43-6.

Frisch, Otto R. "The Los Alamos Experience." *New Scientist*, vol. 83 (July 19, 1979): 186-88.

Groves, Leslie R. "Development of the Atom Bomb." *The Military Engineer*, vol. 38 (June 1946): 233-43.

Gruber, Carol S. "Manhattan Project Maverick: The Case of Leo Szilard." *Prologue*, vol. 15 (Summer 1983): 73-87.

Hunner, Jon. "Family Secrets: The Growth of Community at Los Alamos." *New Mexico Historical Review*, vol. 72 (January 1997): 39-46.

McDaniel, Boyce. "A Physicist at Los Alamos." *Bulletin of the Atomic Scientists*, vol. 30 (December 1974): 39-43.

McKibbin, Dorothy. "109 East Palace Avenue." *LASL News*, vol. 5 (June 28, 1963): 6-7.

Manley, Kathleen E.B. "Women of Los Alamos During World War II: Some of their Views." *New Mexico Historical Review*, vol. 65 (April 1990): 251-66.

Norris, Margot. "Dividing the Indivisible: The Fissured Story of the Manhattan Project." *Cultural Critique*, vol. 35 (Winter   1996-97): 5-38.

Dissertation:

Chambers, Marjorie Bell. "Technically Sweet Los Alamos: The Development of a Federally Sponsored Scientific Community." Unpublished Ph.D. dissertation, University of New Mexico, 1974.

INDEX